Using An Offshore Bank For Profit, Privacy and Tax Protection

by Jerome Schneider

Third edition ISBN 0-933560-03-6

Published by
WFI Corporation
357 S. Robertson Blvd.
Beverly Hills, CA 90211 (213) 855-1000

Trade discounts available on 25 or more copies.

TABLE OF CONTENTS

Using An Offshore Bank For Profit, Privacy and Tax Protection

Introduction

"Every man, as long as he does not violate the laws of justice, is left perfectly free to pursue his own interest in his own way, and to bring forth his industry and capital into competition with those of any other man, or order of men."

—Adam Smith
The Wealth of Nations

If Adam Smith were alive today, I would have asked his advice before tackling this book. Although his work was first published over 200 years ago, its message remains a haunting concern for most contemporary financial thinkers. And his vision of a free nation—where men and women enjoy the right to determine their own destinies—continues to guide me as I re-read my manuscript and search for its overriding themes.

Like many of my professional associates, and along with innumerable investors around the world, I am concerned about the everyday encroachments on freedom. Perhaps it is only idealism that suggests freedom brings with it responsibility. But as Americans this is our legacy. And it is worth preserving.

One thing seems certain: there can be no label of freedom hung on any nation that fails to ensure the financial autonomy of its citizens. Without the inherent right to do with our property whatever we wish, we live under the weight of undue political restraint. For U.S. citizens, bureaucratic interference has become a formidable reality. But we remain free to combat it. Frustrated and angry, we openly argue against the excessive taxation that chips away at our earnings. We attempt to guard against the advanced technology that creeps further into the privacy of our banking affairs. And members of every social class continue to work toward the luxury of affluence.

In other countries, financial freedom is not a subject for such public debate. Elsewhere, it is a matter no longer private—but made blatantly the domain of government authority. Not long ago, the world received news that Mexico had nationalized its banks. With that headline, I was immediately reminded of an old client, Jose Vasquez Beltran. A well-established Mexican producer, Beltran has made films with some of his country's most celebrated stars. As a result, he has acquired a considerable net worth.

In the spring of 1981, Beltran attended one of my firm's investment seminars. Afterwards, we met for a private consultation and I learned that he was eager to move his money into the U.S. banking system. Anxious about his country's economic uncertainty, leery of the continued devaluation of the peso, and already attuned to the vague possibility of nationalization, Beltran sought a way of insuring his life's earnings. I realize now, even more acutely than I did then, that he had a premonition of things to come. More important, he had the courage to act on his intuition.

As we got to know each other and exchanged stories of mutual interest, it became clear that he was familiar with offshore banking. He had taken it upon himself to investigate its benefits, and found in the idea of establishing his own private facility some distant hope of refuge. For Beltran, offshore banking offered a practical solution to very real problems. I imagine that today he is extremely happy with himself. And proud of having taken decisive steps to protect his assets. While many of his compatriots are left to stew in an economic crisis that threatens their security, Beltran's wealth is safely on account in his own offshore bank.

It is partly due to government actions the world around that I have written this book. Mexico was not the first country to nationalize its banking system. It probably won't be the last. Which one will be next? And how many individuals will wring their hands in regret only after it is too late to make a difference? Questions like these lead to disquieting conclusions, and they should encourage investors everywhere to guarantee that they are "left perfectly free."

In short, this is a book intended for people ready to act. It is written in response to freedoms lost, but simultaneously in praise of the many more we still enjoy. Sometimes I speak of the negative, but more often I attempt to address the encompassing opportunities that remain at every doorstep. For people who can seize those opportunities, this will be a book of calculated strategy.

It is also a book for the painfully fearful. As we move through the 1980s, it seems that many investors are growing apprehensive about their economic security. I have talked with hundreds of people—here and abroad—whose faith in traditional forms of investment has begun to crumble. They worry that their currencies will break under the financial strain of the next few years, and doubt their governments' abilities to cope with pressing, perhaps insoluble, economic strife. Caught between the immobilization that comes with uncertainty and the isolation resulting from government indifference, they are desperately looking for asset protection and investment profit. For all of them, I hope to offer words of encouragement and present a guide to practical and fruitful action. In the most basic sense, this is a how-to book. On the surface, it shows you ways in which to organize a private offshore bank. Below the surface, it is a how-to on economic security and profitability.

Essentially, there is nothing startling about the notions underlying the text. After all, banks have traditionally functioned as financial intermediaries. They have historically brought lenders and borrowers together, helping each in a different way. Wealthy families, groups of rich individuals, and major companies have often found themselves able to open and operate a domestic bank. What makes this book unusual is its suggestion that moderately successful citizens can now afford to follow suit.

Each month, I meet people who at one time would have been frozen out of the banking business, but by utilizing the simple principles of offshore banking, they have learned to creatively unlock the door to opportunities once reserved exclusively for the ultrarich. In many cases, they decide to form a personal bank in one of several foreign jurisdictions—places where they can enjoy complete confidentiality, freedom from taxation, and sensible regulation. This book is about their "discovery."

My primary objective is to introduce you to a whole new world. You will find an introduction to and an explanation of offshore banking. For the headstrong, I have even included a step-by-step approach to purchasing your first facility.

I will also take you behind the scenes and into the lives of several clients in the process of operating their own offshore institutions.

The text that follows is my own, but its themes and stories come from associates, clients, and advisors who have encouraged me to put it down in black and white. The time seemed right. So, with thanks to friends, here it is. With literary imperfections and sporadic sweeps of inspiration, I hope the work will serve to nudge all readers into the thrill of action.

Clearly, there is no book that can adequately substitute for professional advice. But if I can propel you into a personal investigation of offshore banking's benefits, I will be more than satisfied with the effort. I can promise that after a careful reading, you will be ready to ask the right questions. More important, you will have an insight into a dazzling world that I am pleased to have made my own. Perhaps, one day, you will make it yours.

Jerome Schneider

CHAPTER 1

INTRODUCING OFFSHORE BANKING

James Tillar recently came into a rather substantial inheritance. His great-aunt had never confided the extent of her affection, so news that she had willed him $100,000 came as quite a surprise. So far, Jim has purchased a brand-new, jet-black Porsche (with every imaginable extra), an entire wardrobe of Armani suits, and a backyard Jacuzzi. Not to appear selfish, he bought his girlfriend a beautiful emerald ring and 12 dozen long-stemmed red roses—delivered to her office suite. It's been great fun. But now what?

He would like to invest in something secure, something that will reap profits over time, but he is looking for a sense of financial adventure. He likes to travel and has been abroad several times, but doesn't have the international contacts that lead to lucrative investment opportunity. With just a little more than $65,000 to spend, Jim has been caught offguard. His girlfriend constantly warns him that keeping the money in a savings account is both a waste of time and a steady drain on his capital. But he knows of no viable alternative. Maybe he'll just take off for Morocco, a retired man of leisure, and take up residence in some deserted Casbah . . . .

Mike Kastin still remembers when his father worked sixteen hours a day, six days a week, and reserved every Sunday to worry about his family's financial future. But about ten years ago, the hard work began to pay off. The small construction company his father owned suddenly caught on, and before long he was one of the most respected contractors in Minneapolis. With money coming in, he made a select number of real-estate investments, began a trust for Mike and his sister, and opened the first French-style cafe in the city. All his investments proved good ones, and today his combined assets total nearly $4 million. Mike will be stepping into more and more of his father's professional commitments over the next few years. The career possibility excites him, but he is concerned about the staggering tax load imposed not only on his family's personal income but on their investment income as well. His goal—for himself, his sister, and his parents—is to devise a creative alternative.

Neither of these scenarios should seem absurd. Each of them is representative of many Americans who find themselves caught in a maze of both financial confusion and challenge. This book is for them—to serve as a realistic guide through the many life choices that can be made within that maze. I will attempt to offer a clear explanation of what I consider to be their best choice—offshore banking.

In the most basic sense, offshore banking is the movement of money across international lines. In practice, it allows the wise investor to synchronize the benefits of various banking activities and blend them into a unique, tax-saving, and profitable financial strategy. For the careful and conscientious individual, offshore banking is one of the most pragmatic ways to expand a universe of financial opportunity because it is one of the most creative ways of diversifying assets.

Still, there is an important difference between knowing that you must devise an investment program and actually putting one into practice. People with sizable assets to protect are repeatedly urged to formulate a personal financial strategy. Inevitably, they find themselves inundated with literature and suggestions about this tax haven or that, the benefits and liabilities of a Swiss bank account, and even the possibility of borrowing funds abroad. It can be a confusing process of sorting through options. But it's well worth the effort because knowledge, as they say, is power. For those willing to seize the moment, the 1980s can be years of profit and success. Let others accentuate the negative. The alert investor surveys the international marketplace and, above all, spies opportunity and potential gain.

Whether living in this country or in another, the wise investor seeks to assume responsibility for his money. In the context of today's economic uncertainties, inaction may result in loss. Words like "savings," "security," and even "banking" have taken on new meaning in the past twenty years. At one time, it was possible to relax in the knowledge that you had money in the bank and ample enough shares of reliable stock to ensure you and your family a lifetime of security. But, at one time, to have earned a million dollars by the time you were thirty was reason enough to get your picture in a business magazine. Times have changed, and today you run the risk of seeing your assets stagnate or devalue unless you do something to activate them. If this book communicates only one thing, I would have it be a clear message that passivity in personal finance implies no gain. Financial success necessitates that you become actively involved in your own financial planning. And it demands that you stay involved.

The right moves come with experience and from a well-advised awareness of investment strategy. Without background knowledge, you are prone to act in ways which negate your own best interests. If you realize that some action is necessary but fail to master the myriad factors that affect your decisions, you are sure to chase one false start after another. And your search for the perfect plan—one that offers enormous profit, total privacy, and absolutely no risk—will turn into a hunt for the lost needle in an imaginary haystack.

Every sound financial program I have ever outlined for a client or learned about from an associate has balanced the various aspects of investment and, more important, placed them in their proper perspective. I have worked with some clients who were so risk-averse that they happily relinquished probable profit to avoid even the remote possibility of loss. On the other hand, I have known investors who have taken measured risks when they felt there was a good chance to profit substantially. In essense, there is no financial plan capable of pleasing everyone. You will gain from international finance only if you accept from the start that your investment strategy must be designed to meet your particular needs and no one else's.

Fortunately, there are many people here and abroad who have weighed these issues for themselves. A great percentage of them agree that offshore banking is a safe, viable, and lucrative alternative to the less appealing environment that predominates in the U.S. Based on their experience and on the advice of financial experts worldwide, it seems fair to say that offshore banking could be the first step to your financial freedom.

What Is Offshore Banking?

Perhaps the most important thing to be said about offshore banking is that it offers an all-encompassing financial approach. Whatever your current financial needs, offshore banking can provide you with an intelligent, practical alternative to the vexing problems of personal, business, and corporate money management. It can also meet your need to conduct financial transactions in a private environment, free of overly burdensome government rules and regulations.

Offshore banks are, quite simply, financial institutions situated outside the United States. Because they don't operate within the U.S., they are rarely subject to our state or federal laws. Banks located in the Bahamas, Cayman Islands, Netherland Antilles, Montserrat, Singapore, Vanuatu or, most recently, the Mariana Islands are considered "offshore" banks. As such, they are able to offer a wide range of services well beyond the legal capability of domestic banks. They allow you to increase your profits, reduce your taxes, and raise money at lower interest rates—all while you legally escape stringent domestic red tape.

Offshore banks are chartered under the laws of the country in which they operate, and are fully recognized within the international banking community. They constitute today's most desirable haven to protect your money from inflation, from dollar devaluation, from the tax collector, and from your creditors. As the surest signal of their strategic advantage, there has been a 43-percent increase in the growth of offshore banking in the last decade. In the Caribbean alone, dollar deposits in offshore American banks jumped from about $25 billion in 1973 to $145 billion in 1980.

Offshore banking is not a recent trend. The Bank of England actually adapted it in 1965 from the Swiss model. At that time,

the Bahama Islands were experiencing severe economic problems; more money was leaving than was flowing in. Because
the Bahamas were technically considered a colony of Great
Britain, the Bank of England was asked to step in and help
resolve the situation. After research and analysis, bank
authorities suggested that the government create a two-tier
banking system: one for local currencies and another for
foreign monies. The onshore banks would serve resident
citizens while the offshore system would work to meet the
banking needs of foreign investors. Aware that wealth
historically has flown through money centers unencumbered
by government controls, island officials decided to attract
money from all of Western Europe and the United States, offering foreign investors a permanent tax holiday, ironclad
secrecy laws, and relaxed banking regulations. In exchange,
they would look forward to an influx of capital and ask for
a license fee.

The financial marriage of island need and customer convenience enjoyed an impressive honeymoon. By 1966, a number
of offshore banking centers had emerged. Several American
banks saw in the Bahamas a golden opportunity to escape
the Federal Reserve's crushing regulations. For their part, a
number of multinational corporations looked upon the foreign
financial centers as the means to a profitable end. They
established their own offshore banking subsidiaries, tapped
into the billion-dollar Eurodollar market, and earned a
substantial interest, which they used to finance domestic
operations.

Offshore dealings simultaneously allowed these American
corporations to avoid heavy U.S. regulations, exchange currency without restriction, shift investments without taxation,
and operate in an environment of complete financial privacy.
By 1973, 156 separate American banks operated in the Caribbean. Continental Oil, Seagram's, Boeing, Firestone and Dow
Chemical all had their own offshore banks.

It didn't take long for other offshore jurisdictions to identify a good thing. Responding to the Bahamas' example,

Switzerland liberalized its banking laws. So did the Cayman Islands. Then came Panama and Hong Kong. In the span of just a few years, a multibillion-dollar industry was born.

But in 1974, the Eurodollar market suffered a major setback—partly as the result of a too liberal and unregulated environment. The collapse of Germany's Bankhaus I.D. Herstatt weakened public confidence, and a number of international investors looked to the U.S. for banking security. They found themselves pressed to tolerate government regulation in exchange for investment and deposit protection under the law. Their departure from the foreign banking network propelled the Eurodollar market into a period of significant change. As if out of nowhere, it became a speculator's marketplace. For the first time, powerful banking institutions were forced to cater to foreign clients. In such a competitive environment, survival meant compromise. The offshore banks that survived were those that offered the highest interest rates and the best returns on initial deposits.

Offshore banking had no choice but to circumvent some rather formidable impediments to international business activity. Lending restrictions, investment limitations, transaction-reporting requirements, public disclosure of records, and licensing of banking operations were all relaxed by eager offshore banking jurisdictions. In the process, an entirely new set of financial concerns became operative. International companies and individual investors seeking access to the specialized resources of the world's financial community—from entree and exclusive capital markets to wholesale borrowing and reduced transaction fees—found that offshore banking met real business priorities. And, as a kind of bonus, it offered the distinction and prestige associated with international banking.

Most important, offshore banking made good business sense. Just as international oil companies often choose to register their ships in an offshore jurisdiction so as to take full advantage of foreign licensing practices, financiers find that offshore banking allows them to conduct business within the legal parameters of a more profit-conducive environment. Like medical research specialists who prefer to explore the possible benefits of Laetrile in foreign countries, where their work remains protected from prohibitive regulation, concerned businessmen find that offshore banking allows them the benefits of foreign investment without constant government supervision.

Ending Misconceptions

Given the current state of our economy and the urgent need among many Americans to avoid excessive taxation, financial red tape, and the unwarranted invasion of privacy, major corporations and individual investors are increasingly becoming attracted to the notion of offshore banking. Their combined enthusiasm has given rise to a relatively young but nonetheless impressive global industry. The Morgan Guaranty Trust has in fact estimated total offshore assets at $1.5 trillion.

Still, the general public remains grossly uninformed. Most people who have heard about offshore banking associate it with legendary "paper pirates" who pass a flow of bogus money from shell banks in the Caribbean. Or they think of fraudulent users who issue phony checks and letters of credit. These scandals hide the positive nature of offshore banking behind a gaudy mask of sensationalism. The truth is, many prestigious U.S. banks maintain offshore operations. The Bank of America, Chase Manhattan Bank, Citibank, N.A., Chemical Bank, The First National Bank of Chicago, Morgan Guaranty Trust, and scores of other financial institutions around the world have become an integral part of this burgeoning industry.

The legitimacy of offshore banking can be further underscored by the fact that some of the most respected names in American business conduct their banking outside the United States: Sears, Boeing, Firestone, Continental Oil, Seagram's, Exxon, Monsanto, Rockwell International, and Fluor to name just a few. (A more complete list of offshore users and bankers would be nearly impossible to obtain because most foreign jurisdictions prohibit the disclosure of shareholder or apparent owner information. These companies, however, are public corporations. As such, they must disclose their holdings in an annual 10K report filed with the Securities and Exchange Commission.)

So, if you are at all familiar with offshore banking, you are among America's financial avant-garde. For obvious reasons, foreign financial centers are prohibited from advertising in U.S. media. As a result, very little information has been available—except to the most sophisticated corporations with international expertise and well-informed legal staffs. But within the past few years (and as a result of important offshore policy changes), small- to medium-sized companies and individual investors have begun to contemplate the possibilities of offshore banking. Almost inevitably, those willing to investigate its opportunities find that far from an illegal or even clandestine activity, offshore banking is a widely utilized, attractive alternative to onshore banking. Moreover, it is a remarkably profitable way of doing business.

Since virtually anyone can benefit from an involvement in offshore banking, it would be difficult to identify the one particular individual or investment consortium that stands to gain the most. There is the real-estate, commodities, or securities investor who has grown tired of paying taxes on his profits and gains. There are people who want their investments and other financial transactions cloaked in absolute secrecy. I have worked with entrepreneurs who have considered offshore banking a way of combining large profits with a bit of business adventure. Often times, loan and mortgage brokers are attracted to offshore activity because it allows them to legally lend at interest rates that exceed onshore restrictions. And, of course, there is the person who wants to legally avoid a heavy tax load.

Sometimes, people find that one specific aspect of their financial portfolio calls for offshore dealings. For instance, conscientious executives occasionally learn that a particular transaction results in the least amount of confusion, expense, and red tape if it is negotiated outside the country. Or a company may decide to establish its own offshore bank because it wants to take advantage of check-float time. In essence, offshore banking can offer you impressive interest rates, a tax-lenient environment, and considerable financial privacy. The way in which you can benefit from offshore banking depends entirely upon your personal financial needs.

As a general rule, I have found that people with assets of $150,000 or more will want to bank offshore. If you know you have something to protect, you need the financial benefits of the approach. If you suspect you may have something to protect, you could probably benefit from an offshore involvement. After all, U.S. banks cannot do business with your profit priorities in mind. Even if they were eager to offer the interest and lending advantages you could find abroad, onshore banks would still be subject to strict government regulations limiting their professional autonomy. Every bank operating within the U.S. is under the legal supervision of four separate enforcement agencies. A brief look at each will illustrate the constraints placed on our banking community:

- The Securities and Exchange Commission (SEC) governs the issuance of securities. Although banks are not technically subject to SEC rules for the registration of their securities, they are responsible to the Commission once certificates are issued.

- The Internal Revenue Service (IRS) is responsible for the payment and collection of all federal taxes. Because U.S. banks must pay taxes, they come under constant IRS supervision.

- The Comptroller of Currency or a state's banking department is privy to virtually every facet of the banking industry and assumes full responsibility for all bank practices within its jurisdiction.

- The U.S. Custom Service keeps track of all currency that flows in and out of this country. By law, banks must report to this agency any transaction that involves more than $10,000.

Onshore banks are also watched and monitored by the Federal Deposit Insurance Corporation (FDIC) and the FBI. What's more, in compliance with the Bank Secrecy Act of 1970, they must retain all bank records for a full five-year period—allowing the government to reach back that far in any investigation it may see fit to conduct.

Words to the Wise

Clearly, there is an immediate need for individuals, companies, and commercial institutions to work around complex banking regulations. Offshore banking meets that need because it protects assets from excessive government interference.

With an unpredictable economy breathing down your neck, you cannot afford the luxury of financial passivity. Whether you consider yourself a business magnate or a conservative individual investor, you would be wise to assume responsibility for the assets you control. The moment you walk into an onshore bank to conduct business, you are walking into government red tape, financial disclosures, and income-tax burdens. The fact is, onshore banks cannot escape government scrutiny. But you can.

I admit from the start that there has never been a simple answer to all investment dilemmas. However, I do maintain that offshore banking is today's most comprehensive and intelligent approach to financial planning. With so many options, programs, and offers constantly proposed (each of them purporting to be the ultimate "best plan") it's difficult to choose. But as you try in your own way to sort through the confusion and separate fact from financial fiction, remember that offshore banking assures discerning investors the highest profit, best tax protection and most financial privacy—at the least risk.

CHAPTER 2

HOW OFFSHORE BANKING
CAN WORK FOR YOU

After an initial introduction to offshore banking, some people will ask, "Does it really work?" Yes, it does. And with careful planning, it can work extremely well. In practice, offshore banks serve the needs of all parties involved. They benefit their host countries, typically offer impressive services to their customers, and make their owners financially autonomous.

Just a few years ago, I met a man named Kenneth Shea. He was a registered participant at one of the investment seminars we periodically offer around the country. Initially, Ken seemed like a quiet enough fellow. But as it turned out, he took up a good deal more than his fair share of conference time. Over and over again, he would challenge presentation remarks, and rebuff the various financial strategies proposed by members of the panel.

Finally, between sessions on the second day, I joked with him, asking whether or not friends ever called him Tom for short. Looking every inch the serious businessman, he replied, "No, why do you ask?" Only half jesting, I said, "Because you're quite a doubting Thomas!"

That coffee-break exchange marked the beginning of a long and exceptionally satisfying professional association. Ken not only enlisted my help in establishing his own offshore facility, but continues, even now, to push me for additional banking applications. He is a typical offshore investor in that he began with a set of well-argued questions, asked them one by one, found the answers he needed to hear, and acted on his own best judgment.

Ken's offshore story is an interesting one. But before we review it, let's cover some more background material.

Although offshore banks have been established all over the world, most are located in the Pacific and Caribbean islands. By welcoming offshore investors, these participating jurisdictions find that they enjoy a healthy influx of foreign capital and a pleasant boost in annual tourism. Unemployment is relieved and island economy is strengthened. If, over time, a hosting locale proves itself a reliable financial center, it gains respect and prestige within the international business community. To maintain a good reputation, most jurisdictions diligently attend to the needs of their foreign clientele. That, in turn, attracts more outside investment and the cycle begins again.

For their part, offshore-bank customers can take advantage of island laws governing financial activity. In particular, they can insure against government appropriation of funds, guarantee their financial privacy, and earn substantial interest on their deposits.

But without question, the individuals who own offshore banks gain the most. They position themselves to enjoy all customer advantages in addition to more exclusive benefits. For instance, owning an offshore bank allows you to engage in financial activities reserved only for banks. Specifically, you can raise capital from various sources around the world and reduce borrowing costs.

Whatever your role in a possible offshore venture, keep in mind that offshore banks are not all alike. In fact, one of the most attractive features of offshore banking is its flexibility. Separate institutions are designed to function in distinct ways, and always in accord with the needs of their owners. Imagine them as tailor-made financial facilities created to meet very specific requirements.

If and when you begin to think about offshore banking for yourself, be specific about what you want from the involvement. If your top priority is privacy, you will want to pursue one set of jurisdictional options. If, on the other hand, you are less concerned with privacy than with profit, you will probably want to explore different foreign centers. As a case in point, Mexico offers one of the most confidential banking environments available today. But your assets may not be as secure there as they would be in another locale. So evaluate your personal needs, talk with experts and those who are already banking offshore. Then, make your final decision based on clear images of your own financial strategy. Keep just one "must" in mind: any offshore bank worth owning or doing business with must operate within the legal parameters of the host country.

To understand something about the nature of a proper and legal environment, consider Vanuatu, formerly the New Hebrides. This small Pacific island consciously drafted laws allowing it to function as an internationally preferred tax haven. The government implemented legislation regarding financial secrecy and put into effect specialized banking and business regulations. As a result, Vanuatu imposes no income tax—on residents or on foreign investors. There is no capital-gains, withholding, or sales tax, and no estate duty. The island has no reporting requirement for the movement of funds, no matter their size or frequency.

To safeguard themselves against abusive or fraudulent users, the Vanuatu government has made it somewhat difficult to obtain a private bank on the island. Entry requirements and the mandatory screening process can be long and complex. The island also imposes an annual audit requirement on every company, bank, and insurance firm based within its jurisdiction. Over the years, these rules and regulations have been monitored regularly and carefully to ensure that foreign investors operate within the law.

My point is, offshore banking is not a renegade activity in Vanuatu. It is a legally defined and government-endorsed way of doing business. To secure its position in the international business community, the island government custom-tailors various aspects of its legal system to complement offshore banking priorities. In this way, Vanuatu has become an internationally respected financial center. Without a legal framework, the island would lose investors to more reputable jurisdictions.

By and large, the people involved in offshore banking are responsible individuals concerned about the legal and regulatory profile of any potential financial center. Their objectives include profit, tax protection, and above all, the ability to make private decisions about personal money matters. Offshore banks are carefully structured to address these concerns.

A Preferred Customer

You can utilize an offshore bank in one of two ways: as a customer or as an owner. So, before booking a seat on the next flight to Vanuatu, think about whether you want to become a customer in someone else's bank or acquire your own charter and license. Your decision should be based somewhat on personal preference, but mostly on pragmatic judgment. Realistically, you must take into account the size of your assets. While you can sometimes open an offshore account for as little as $50, you will need at least $25,000 to establish your own offshore bank.

Beyond assets, determine your objectives. As an offshore customer you can look forward to several benefits. For instance, foreign checking accounts pay up to four times as much interest as their U.S. counterparts. Savings accounts pay even more. In addition, an offshore account allows you to borrow at far below the domestic prime interest rate, and your privacy is essentially guaranteed under strict laws protecting financial records from unwarranted inspection. Assets held in an offshore bank are safer than their onshore equivalent because they are immune to judgments, seizures, and writs of execution. And, since many island jurisdictions impose no income tax, your tax burden can be significantly reduced by moving assets abroad. In short, an offshore checking or savings account allows people an opportunity to enjoy real financial benefits while learning the mechanics of a complex business phenomenon. You will need to choose an offshore bank that suits your particular priorities. Generally, you would be best served by a personal introduction. After all, if you learn about a bank from a friend or associate, you will feel that much more confident about the entire venture. Likewise, when a foreign banker meets you through a trusted customer, he will enter the association with fewer reservations. If a personal referral is not possible, you should resign yourself to several weeks of preliminary research.

Your first two decisions are obvious: where do you want to open your account and what bank would best serve your needs? Be methodical in your approach. Updated editions of *The Banker's Almanac and Year Book* and *Polk's World Bank Directory* can be reviewed at most libraries. Both books list all the banks in the world, country by country. They also provide the address and telephone number of each main branch. You can obtain additional information from national embassies. A letter of general query will ordinarily result in a return packet full of brochures and articles concerning the region.

When you have the needed information, choose perhaps ten banks in two or three different jurisdictions. Pick some because they are large and well-respected, others because their names or advertising suggest they are associated with international institutions. And pick one or two just because your intuition tells you that they might be "right." Send to each of them an identical letter. Ask about opening and operating an account with the bank and request that all relevant information be sent you as soon as possible. The replies will be quite useful in making a final decision. Some banks may not reply at all; others are likely to take weeks before getting back to you. Expect some to send prepared information packets with a polite but impersonal cover letter. Hope that you receive a few personal replies that address each point raised in your letter.

By examining all that you receive, you can learn a great deal. Which show a steady growth of Capital Reserves? Are financial statements issued regularly, and are they easily available? How old is each bank? How many of them are old enough to have experience and still young enough to present a financially progressive image? Which have high liquidity ratios and what interest rates do they offer? Interest rates should be competitive, but be wary of interest rates that are too high—they can be a signal that the bank is desperate for business.

Remember that when you're safeguarding your money, it is impossible to gather too much information. Use every conceivable avenue to learn about your final two or three bank options. If your finances permit and you are conservative by nature, visit the last few possibilities on your list. The trip will teach you about the jurisdiction and its people. But, more important, take time to acquaint yourself with the people involved. You can learn more about the bank itself over lunch with the manager than you ever could within the formal confines of an office meeting.

When you make your final decision, your new offshore bank will probably allow you to open the account by mail. It will require the completion of two signature cards and an application form. There will also be a list of bank terms and conditions to be signed and returned. Deposits can be made in cash (if a personal visit is made). By mail, cash is sent by international money order.

Once established, your offshore-bank account will run itself, growing and prospering in the background. It is not necessary to visit the bank or even the offshore jurisdiction. If you prefer, the bank will never even make contact. And, at any time, your account may be closed by mail and all funds transferred elsewhere.

When choosing your offshore jurisdiction, be aware of one other important consideration. In today's world, where fast changes in various financial markets dictate immediate action, instant communication is essential. You must be able to communicate with your offshore representative on a moment's notice in order to ensure a swift, efficient transfer of funds. You should insist on the right to authorize telephone transactions, with the understanding that your calls will be followed by a formal letter of confirmation.

If you plan to use your account frequently, you will want the luxury of telex; it's fast, accurate, and extremely safe, as it allows you to keep your money in a corresponding FDIC-insured account in the U.S. By utilizing the telex system, your transactions involve nothing more than electronic signals sent from one banking jurisdiction to another. In practical terms, your assets are maintained in one of the world's large money centers. (For U.S. investors, deposits usually remain in a New York or Los Angeles bank. For Europeans, funds are typically held in London.) These large and internationally established institutions enjoy a symbiotic relationship with one another and use a debit-and-credit method for transferring money on behalf of their clients.

For example, if you want to transfer $100,000 to the Eurodollar market, you can issue a check on account in a New York bank, payable to a payee in Europe. The New York bank wires your funds to a London center with instructions to credit you, their U.S. customer. In this way, your banking instructions are carried out without actual currency ever being sent abroad.

Ownership: Ultimate Control

In addition to these customer conveniences, offshore-bank owners stand to gain other attractive benefits. By acquiring your own offshore charter and license you can legally operate an entire bank according to your personal priorities. You can lend to third parties, make private investments, accept deposits, initiate trust activity, purchase real estate at low interest, transfer currency at your discretion, offer your customers back-to-back loans, acquire optional/merger funding, and tap into escrow funds for short-term interest gain. I could go on, but suffice it to say that the benefits available to bank owners substantially outweigh the advantages of most other investment vehicles.

At this point, you may be wondering how noncurrency assets move into and out of offshore banks. Real estate, securities, commodities, bullion, personal property, receivables, notes, and contracts may be placed in an offshore bank in several different ways. Despite common assumption, assets need not be physically offshore in order to be owned by the bank. An offshore bank, like any corporation, has a distinct and separate legal status. And it is this status that gives rise to the facility's real benefits. When you transfer the right, title, or interest to any asset, you have technically transferred the asset itself offshore. But even after such a transfer is made, the asset may be repatriated without consequences—provided it has not appreciated.

If you have considerable assets, you may decide to open what we normally think of as a bank, complete with a customary vault, window tellers, and clerks. If you have less money to invest, you may opt for what is termed a 'B' bank, or a "brass-plate" bank. The latter has no walk-in facilities or a street presence, and is often a single office in a multibank complex. Its existence is noted by a simple brass plate on the building exterior and by the services of a resident agent who handles all offshore business by mail, phone, telex, and telecopier.

These offshore banks are composed of five basic elements: the bank charter and license, a resident agent, registered office, a board of directors, and shareholders. I call these prerequisites the "five easy pieces," and they are essential to any offshore banking facility.

- A bank's charter and license work in tandem to outline the institution's basic legal structure. When I speak of the bank charter, I am actually referring to its articles of incorporation and bylaws. This charter lets the host government know how your bank will operate and what its powers will be. In turn, the bank license constitutes jurisdictional approval of the charter. This formal document is the single most important element of any offshore bank, representing the legal endorsement you require and allowing your bank to function in the offshore tax haven.

- You will also need a resident agent who lives in the host country. He will process all your transactions and act as a liaison between you and his foreign government.

- Typically, the resident agent works in a registered office with a telephone, telex, and telecopier. Most registered offices and the majority of resident agents serve more than one offshore bank. But each has its own separate integrity as a financial institution.

- An offshore bank needs a board of directors, all of whom reside outside the United States. According to the IRS, an offshore bank is legally "foreign" only if the location of its management is foreign. Simply put, a legally operating offshore bank has a board of directors (generally made up of one to ten people, all non-U.S. citizens living outside the U.S.).

- The final component of an offshore bank is its shareholders, and they constitute a distinct category. They can be U.S. citizens or even U.S. corporations. Chances are, you will want to serve as majority shareholder, but it is not necessary that you do so. You may prefer to have your attorney or accountant fulfill this function.

Given the fact that so many people are involved, you may wonder who has ultimate control over the venture. Are you in charge, or can the board of directors function independent of your wishes? Let's say you wish to transact an item of business—perhaps you want to issue a loan or accept a deposit. You ask your offshore board of directors, through your resident agent, to approve the transaction. The board meets and, again through the resident agent, conveys its approval—in full accordance with your original directive. Clearly, you hold legal authority to carry out the wishes of the directors, and your transaction is accomplished.

Communication between a shareholder and his offshore board of directors can take various forms. You can work through the mail, but packages generally run from four to seven days between the West Coast and the Caribbean basin. Telex is much faster, and it is possible to work with a code so that only you, your resident agent, and your board know what is being said. You can also use a telecopier that will actually transmit a one-page document in six minutes. With this method you could, for example, spend just fifteen minutes to send a loan request to the board, which would meet, grant approval to issue funds for the loan, sign the loan document, and telecopy approval so that funds could be issued here in the United States. Finally, you can opt for telephone communication, but do consider relevant time-zone differentials. If you acquire an offshore bank somewhere in the Far East or in the South Pacific, you are working within the imits of a nineteen-hour time difference.

One side point is worth mentioning. If you are seriously considering the idea of owning your own offshore bank, you will want to decide whether to purchase an already established bank or to start your own. Each approach has its advantages, but if you are a busy entrepreneur for whom time is money, it may be more practical to purchase an already existing bank. It will save you an enormous amount of preliminary work.

You should realize that for all the relative ease that offshore banking can offer, you are still thinking about a very complex business venture. It can sometimes appear manageable, and many beginners feel confident that they are capable of mastering the details on their own. Nevertheless, I would urge you to seek professional advice and assistance when making decisions about your offshore endeavors.

To help ease the burden of legally conducting business offshore, specialized management companies have been formed. Their services can provide you with the sophistication you need in order to compete on an international scale. A competent and experienced consultant will serve as a welcome source of business support, keeping you updated on the fast-changing aspects of offshore banking and providing nominee officers and directors. In short, a qualified consultant will make certain all possible offshore benefits are delivered and preserved.

A Case in Point

With an understanding of these basic techniques, you are ready for a simple case study. For the purposes at hand, let's talk again about my old friend, Ken Shea. At the time we met, Ken was a full-time investor living in Palm Springs. He was heavily involved in California real estate, as well as in securities and commodities. We talked at length about his financial portfolio, and after thinking through options for a few weeks he decided to establish an offshore bank facility in St. Vincent. His objective was extremely straightforward: he wanted to reduce and, if possible, eliminate U.S. taxes on his assets. He was also eager to raise capital by attracting deposit customers, because the more capital he raised from third parties, the stronger his contention that the bank was in the banking business (an important consideration, given U.S. tax law); deposit capital could be used to increase the size of his personal investment portfolio while it obligated him to repay only a fixed rate of return; and if he could secure depositors, he would acquire customers to whom he might eventually offer more sophisticated banking services.

Ken's offshore bank is called The International Security Bank Ltd. (ISB). It has a post-office-box mailing address, a resident agent, offshore directors to manage the facility, and a corresponding FDIC-insured account maintained in Los Angeles, for which Ken is the sole signatory. According to the minutes of the bank, he has been named special advisor to ISB. This official title gives him ongoing authority to perform certain bank activities. For instance, he can plan new business strategies and explore creative investment possibilities.

In late 1979, Ken wrote an advertisement to attract depositors and had it placed in the international edition of *Time*. (The international edition guarantees that it does not have a circulation in the U.S.) In the ad, he offered 17-percent-per-annum tax-free interest on six-month certificates of deposit, and directed interested parties to write for further information. Working out of a brass-plate bank registered office, ISB's resident agent fulfilled all mail requests by sending prospective customers an account opening form and a letter describing the bank's certificates of deposit. The advertisement was unusually successful, and within a matter of several weeks, checks began arriving at the bank's offshore post-office box. Upon receipt, and in accordance with Ken's prearranged instructions, ISB's resident agent confirmed each deposit and sent customers a certificate of deposit.

In one case, ISB received a $5,000 check for a six-month certificate of deposit from Victor Valdez, who, at that time, lived in Chile and wanted his money offshore to protect it from government expropriation. ISB's resident agent promptly deposited the check in a local bank and, after collection, wire-transferred the full amount to Ken's California-based account. It was journaled in ISB's ledgers—both offshore and in Los Angeles—as a loan. Finally, at his discretion as special advisor, Ken invested the money in securities, commodities, and real estate.

Clearly, the *Time* advertisement helped develop business for ISB. It amounted to a solicitation that did not infringe on U.S. tax or banking statutes, and it enhanced ISB's reputation as a bank doing business with third parties. Valdez met his needs by successfully expatriating assets from a repressive government. The money was held in accordance with Ken's mandated procedures, and easily found its way back to him in the United States. Most important, this transaction, repeated again and again, built an impressive customer list for the facility's future financial activity.

By mid-1981, ISB had established itself as a responsible offshore bank. And Ken began to think about expanding his scope of operation. Frankly, it took a bit of time for him to gain the necessary confidence. But eventually, I convinced him of the potential profits contained in his mailing list. Just a few months ago, we worked with a small, professional team of free-lance writers and designers to prepare an in-depth brochure describing the many sophisticated investment services (safe deposit, trust services, and precious-metal trading, etc.) offered by ISB.

At this writing, the printed brochures have been air-freighted to Ken's resident agent. Within weeks they will have been mailed to ISB's entire customer list. Although we won't know the outcome for a few months, I have told Ken to expect several potential clients to write back, expressing interest in an expanded association with ISB. Meetings should be scheduled with those indicating a substantial interest. And assured that he can secure business, Ken should plan a short trip overseas to meet with new clients. My guess is that by using this method, he will find his investment opportunities to be virtually unlimited. He may even decide to discreetly approach U.S. customers who, through a mutual contact, have heard about ISB services.

The simplicity of this example is not exaggerated. Like many other offshore bankers, Ken is apt to find his offshore bank facility a veritable Aladdin's lamp. Customers like Valdez will continue to enjoy the security of a bank account safe from government interference. More adventuresome clients will be offered more expanded conveniences. And, as a bank owner, Ken will reap the many benefits of a tax haven, ensure his own financial privacy, gain the opportunity to creatively invest substantial sums of money, and live with the prestige of operating his own international bank.

CHAPTER 3

THE BENEFITS OF OFFSHORE BANKING

Just before the outbreak of World War II, Lance Lubeck fled Berlin. Like many other German refugees, he left suddenly and landed in the United States without money or a destination. Fortunately, he had managed over the years to move 20,000 German marks into a Swiss bank. Lubeck's foresight served him well. Once in the U.S., he sent for the offshore money and started a new life with some degree of financial security.

Political instability and persecution outlived the millions of Lance Lubecks who could not get out of Nazi Germany. Every day, people around the world attempt to escape repressive dictatorships, violent revolutions, and brutal oppression. As U.S. citizens, we face far less dramatic political abuse. But, even here, the wisest individuals plan for the unforeseen.

If nothing else, the 1980s promise an economic challenge. We live in a time when anything can happen. Only the naive investor willingly stakes a life's savings on the national economy. For all intents and purposes, the steel industry is dead; the auto industry is dying, and recent reports suggest that even U.S. banks are facing real threats to their survival. With these bulwarks of American industry in jeopardy, it seems a good time to act with careful forethought.

Even the most encouraging projections indicate it will take years to turn the economy around. It would be unwise to wait for the recovery. You should place your assets where they will most benefit you and your family. An offshore-bank involvement prepares you for the unexpected. Even more important, it allows you the peace of mind that comes from knowing your financial strategy has taken into account the vagaries of a stalled economy.

Aside from preparing for contingencies, alert investors should position themselves to take immediate advantage of foreign investments. If you keep all your assets in the U.S., you will not be able to capitalize fast enough on future offshore opportunities. Unless you have diversified your assets—

either through an offshore account or by acquiring your own offshore bank—you run the risk of stewing in the same pot as all other disgruntled onshore customers. Essentially, it is a matter of spreading your assets so as to limit your risks. Even a small offshore account covers you in case of sudden economic change. It ensures your financial privacy in the face of proliferating data-base information systems, and offers you an amazing array of banking services.

Americans perceive banking in limited terms. Perhaps because we have never learned to expect true customer convenience, we do not turn to our bankers for personalized or sophisticated service. Time and again, clients who have opened an offshore account or who have established their own brass-plate facility will comment on the almost old-fashioned concern that is paid to their money matters.

To be fair, there are still a few private banks in this country that offer affluent customers the red-carpet treatment, but such institutions are fast becoming extinct. Offshore banks, on the other hand, are designed for across-the-board convenience. They can offer you everything from savings accounts and commodities exchange to money-market investments and Eurocurrency loans—all under one roof.

The Eight Main Reasons

People utilize offshore banks for various reasons. Depending upon the breadth of your portfolio, your taste for investment adventure, and your strategic money needs, offshore banking will result in varying advantages and conveniences. In theory, it can offer you benefits ranging from a quiet sense of financial security to the excitement of internationally sophisticated investment opportunity. When I counsel people considering this new banking option, I focus on eight main incentives for moving assets offshore. What follows is a brief summary of each.

High Interest Rates. Domestic banks are, by law, prohibited from paying any more than 5 1/4 percent on deposits. These institutions would like to pay more but are barred from doing so by federal regulations. Offshore banks, on the other hand, can pay whatever rate of interest they deem appropriate. Some offer 20 percent on checking accounts and even more on savings accounts.

Financial Privacy. Strict offshore secrecy laws legally shield your banking records from unwarranted probes and aggressive competitors. If you are ever involved in a lawsuit—whether as the person being sued or as an angry creditor forced to sue someone else—your onshore checks, bank records, and correspondence, copies of your loan applications, and even deposit slips are open to inspection and seizure. By banking offshore, you prevent any such possibility. As has been indicated, most foreign jurisdictions have intentionally enacted laws to protect the confidentiality of your financial records. In many locales, banks are legally prohibited from divulging this sort of information, irrespective of the circumstances.

Tax Protection. Offshore financial centers have earned an international reputation because they function as legal tax havens. Many investors find, in fact, that tax protection (for dividends, interest, and royalties) is paramount to their financial strategy. These offshore customers and owners have done nothing more than come to a reasonable conclusion: why allow investment income to be taxed when offshore banking can prevent it?

Immunity to Domestic Law. Every American business is subject to domestic law and regulation. Over the years, large U.S. companies have constantly bemoaned the drudgery of a complex, slow-moving, bureaucratic legal system that limits their ability to operate at top efficiency for the least amount of money. Increasing numbers of them are beginning to do something about it. Certain sectors of the business community have joined powerful single investors in offshore efforts to eliminate unnecessary legal and regulatory restraints. For example, as SEC filings have become increasingly complicated, a number of "captive" insurance companies have been formed outside the United States. Many of these offshore operations are situated in the Bahamas, where companies can circumvent overly restrictive regulation. Offshore mutual funds are also established, simply to avoid SEC and IRS involvement. In a similar fashion, several offshore medical schools are now in operation, designed for students wanting to avoid the inhibitive entry requirements mandated by the American Medical Association.

Asset Protection. Have you ever been haunted by the fear that your checking account will be closed and all your checks returned? It can certainly happen. The U.S. Congress deliberately passed legislation allowing creditors (armed with an attachment order) to freeze and seize your assets—in many cases without your knowledge. But assets placed in an offshore bank are immune to all judgments, seizures, and other judicial writs.

Know, too, that when you place your assets in an offshore bank, you make them virtually invisible to our domestic monetary system. For one thing, these banks maintain a nonresident-alien tax status that enables them to invest and borrow U.S. funds even without a federal or state tax identification number. On a more subtle level, bank ownership is not typically associated with individuals. This country is not yet accustomed to the notion that an entire bank can be just one person.

Inflation Protection. I hate to make adamant statements about inflation. One year it can seem our national nemesis; the next year, we hear it is subsiding. As this is written, the government is instituting measures to reduce inflation, but the efforts are little more than a temporary solution to a long-term problem. By banking offshore, investors obtain a real hedge against inflation because they are at liberty to use currencies other than the U.S. dollar.

Asset Diversification. In this country, Latin America and Western Europe, people are losing their assets—either by theft, seizure, or liens. Offshore-bank customers and owners haven't run this risk. They have carefully taken their nesteggs, spread them out in several foreign jurisdictions, and assured the relative security of their money.

Bank Ownership with a Minimum of Red Tape. If you want to become a U.S. banker, you must have considerable banking experience. You must meet very specific and stringent banking requirements, and must be able to prove that you carry the proper management personnel. And, even if you do enter this inner sanctum, you will be forced to abide by harsh lending limitations and allowed to invest only in circumscribed areas.

You can obtain an offshore banking charter and license with far less experience. In most cases, your past business background will suffice. Moreover, owning an offshore bank will allow you to involve yourself in a number of financial ventures. For instance, it will permit you to make loans (to yourself and other customers), or to decide that your bank should own a car, boat, and/or an airplane.

Beyond a solution to banking red tape, offshore facilities can be fully established for far less money than their domestic counterparts. To acquire a bank in the United States, you may well need between $2 million and $10 million. Compare this to the $25,000 that can establish an offshore bank in many offshore jurisdictions, and then decide for yourself which appears to be the more attractive alternative.

There are, of course, other reasons for becoming involved in an offshore banking venture. Only the specifics of your lifestyle and the limits of your financial portfolio can determine the uses to which you may put an offshore account, or even your own brass-plate bank. Again, as you explore the full range of conveniences available, I urge you to consult with a professional management firm. The cost of hiring a seasoned staff of executives will be more than compensated by the expanded banking services they help you devise.

Getting Specific

There are more than a thousand offshore banks in operation today. The majority of these institutions—whatever their size or location—seek to preserve the same tax protections and eliminate similar business restrictions. In that vein, they

tend to offer many of the same customer services. Access
to the Euro and petrodollar markets, availability of loans
(even to borrowers who might not meet domestic lending
guidelines), trustee services for trusts of every imaginable
description, affordable insurance funds, and transfer pricing all constitute specific offshore bank conveniences. And
they are just a few of the reasons why U.S. banks find it
difficult to keep sophisticated investors.

The ability to raise capital is for many people the biggest
advantage to offshore banking. The reasoning is sound
because an offshore bank is a very appropriate way to raise
money in the international market. By accepting customer
deposits from all over the world, banks can essentially borrow from the public. In effect, offshore bankers are able to
raise capital under another name. The right to make deposits
in other than U.S. currency is another major reason international investors decide to bank offshore. This is due prin-
cipally to the profit-potential inherent in the process. Consider, for example, that Australian dollars are now yielding
19 percent on 30-day deposits. If an investor leaves his money
in such an account, he stands to earn a handsome profit in
a very short time. Nonetheless, he exposes himself to any
potential movement in exchange rates. So, if you decide to
invest in high-yield deposits, be prepared to regularly assess
exchange fluctuations and discuss with your offshore-bank
manager the advantages of various transfer options. You can
sometimes be surprised by the advice you receive. Consider
another case in point.

The Internal Bank in Vanuatu and Europe once offered
up to 55 percent interest on French francs for 30-day money.
Immediately, Europe panicked, thinking the French franc
might radically devalue. Hasty investors transferred assets
into almost anything, just to leave the franc behind them. Less
frantic investors realized that with 55 percent interest on their
certificates, they could withstand a substantial devaluation
and still come out ahead. Opportunities of this nature seldom
occur to people rigidly confined by U.S. dollar assets. But
by expanding your financial involvements offshore, perspec-

tives change. You gain a broader understanding of other currencies and come to feel at ease with their high-yield potential. In conjunction with offshore banks, offshore insurance companies can choose from among a number of investment options. For instance, banks can provide insurance to their customers, and can help transfer funds from an onshore financial entity to its new offshore insurance arm.

In his helpful book, *How to Form Your Own Tax Haven Company Privately*, S. Clark Thomas neatly defines the nature of captive insurance companies. Usually established by major corporations for tax and nontax reasons, these offshore insurance funds are formed "to insure or reinsure the risk of a group of affiliated corporations." In the process, they save their customers a lot of money. Moreover, "a captive jurisdiction often has the use of premium income for a year before it actually pays any of its premiums for reinsuring the risk." In this way, the insurance company wins a kind of one-year grace period, during which it can use the money to make profitable investments.

This corporate strategy is not new. It was first used nearly twenty-five years ago, but only by a very few multinationals. Then, around 1970, a number of powerful American industries began to suffer huge underwriting losses. Pharmaceutical firms were drained of enormous sums as they were forced to pay huge court settlements brought on by faulty birth-control devices. Practicing physicians were also walloped by an unprecedented number of malpractice suits. Long-established insurance companies simply walked away from the problem, and left former clients to fend for themselves.

In effect, the decision to move assets offshore and to form self-centered insurance companies came not from the desire for cheap coverage, but out of absolute professional necessity. The Boston Medical Association, for example, established its own insurance company as a way of obtaining the malpractice insurance that its members could not find elsewhere.

There is another specialized benefit to be obtained from off-shore bank ownership. For many current and potential off-shore bankers, to own their own bank is to display a hard-earned and well-deserved social status. These people enjoy being able to say, "I own a bank." Even beyond the prestige, these bankers know they have made a wise investment. Each year, it becomes more and more difficult to obtain a bank license—here in the United States or offshore. New laws meant to inhibit offshore investors are proposed every day. People who already own an offshore facility are prepared for the future because, in the most intelligent way possible, they have invested in it.

For the Benefit of Corporations

There are a number of special benefits available to the many corporations that own offshore banks. One such advantage is back-to-back loans, whereby relatively low interest is paid to bank depositors while a somewhat higher interest is charged on loans. The spread between the two constitutes every bank's tax-free profit. Centralized cash management is another convenience available through offshore banking. For a corporation with offices around the world, this particular service can be appealing. It allows the corporation to consolidate idle cash balances from various divisions, establish its own offshore facility, and creatively invest in foreign currency markets. The strategy offers three distinct benefits: higher net earnings for the total group, an income that remains tax-free so long as it remains in the bank, and interest income that could never be earned by any of the divisions individually.

This "pooling" principle can be used by individual investors as well. Many corporations of various natures serve clients with relatively small assets—say $20,000 to $30,000. Taken one by one, none of them could really invest enough to make the effort worthwhile. But, by pooling funds into round lots of a half million or a million dollars, corporations can make meaningful investments in Euro or Asian currency. Likewise, an experienced offshore banker can pull together several "small" investors to achieve the same end.

By using offshore banks, corporations can effectively reduce currency controls and arrange for parallel loans. For example, if an American company doing business in Brazil has an excess of cruzeiros (which it cannot convert into dollars, but wants to transfer into reliable currency), it may opt to have its offshore bank lend those cruzeiros to an interested Brazilian firm. Or it can deposit them indirectly into a multinational offshore bank, and earn reliable interest on the money.

Offshore banking can also help corporations facilitate trade. If you have an offshore bank and are doing business here in the United States, you can issue letters of credit, loans and mortgages. In addition, your offshore bank can function as a third party guarantor to group borrowings within affiliated companies. Sometimes, the offshore bank establishes international status and credibility to such an extent that its credit rating exceeds that of the parent company. In such a case, and with the bank's guarantee on a loan application, the company may be able to reduce even its onshore interest rate.

In short, offshore banking offers a unique amalgam of convenience, service, and investment opportunity. Whether you are interested in the industry as an individual seeking to earn high interest on deposits, as part of a consortium of professional associates attracted to the luxury of a legal tax haven, or as a multinational corporation wanting to diversify and grow even more profitable, offshore banking can more than meet your strategic financial goals. Still, when the complexities are stripped away and we can focus on the essential elements of offshore banking, we find that myriad benefits are reduced to an interlocking triad: profit, privacy and tax protection. Each of them has its own long story.

CHAPTER 4

PROFIT

Experience has taught me that whenever people begin thinking about an offshore involvement, their top priority is profit. In fact, a recently completed research survey confirms what I had guessed for some time: fifty percent of all offshore bank owners cite investment as their original motivation for purchase. Time and again, clients have told me that their investment universe expanded tremendously after they acquired their own charter and license. To a somewhat lesser extent, offshore bank customers find that an international checking or savings account multiplies their chances of financial gain. For instance:

Have you always assumed that the American Express Corporation reaps its impressive profits from the plastic credit it extends to you each month? Wrong—at least, wrong in part. Several years ago, this financial-services conglomerate established an offshore bank in London, with satellite offices in Hong Kong and the Cayman Islands. The American Express International Bank is not used for domestic banking purposes, and it does not maintain offices in the United States. It does, however, provide onshore businesses and financial institutions (as well as foreign governments) with a wide range of international banking services. By doing business with the International Bank, clients enjoy access to short-term working capital, term and project financing, collections, deposits, and money-transfer services. For the record, American Express is hardly martyred in the process. Published reports indicate that between 1976 and 1979, the American Express International Bank returned to its parent company a minimum net profit of $30 million per year. Not bad for a sideline business.

Chances are you won't hear Dow Chemical executives complaining about their offshore bank. Several years ago, this Michigan-based industrial corporation established the Dow Banking Corp. in Switzerland. Its purpose was straightforward: to meet the company's portfolio management needs and to handle various international transactions that would prove too complex for any onshore bank. They made the right move. From 1976 to 1979, Dow Banking showed an average profit of $60 million per year.

What about individual investors? One of my clients has already earned $25 million in commissions through his offshore bank. He began by attracting several sources of capital in Europe and then matching the funds with American banks eager to borrow money abroad. By utilizing his bank as an intermediary agent, he plans to earn nearly $5 million over the next three years.

I have another client who creatively combines business with pleasure. He is an active but retired man who acquired an offshore bank in Vanuatu about three years ago. When he is not touring Europe or the Orient, he spends most of his time at the club. By keeping an ear open to friends who are themselves seeking investment profit, he has brought together several associates and set up three separate banking consortiums. In exchange for a $100,000 certificate of deposit, the International Bank of Vanuatu offers its bank customers revolving credit and tax-free accrued interest on their money.

From every angle, offshore banking would appear to have become one of the most appealing, fun, and profitable financial activities of the decade. Here and abroad, money-making strategies are redesigned daily so that individuals with a flair for investment can capitalize on its many benefits. People looking to increase their holdings and assets with speed and security are coming to see offshore banking as a versatile and complete path to profit.

While other industries confront the problems of inflation and recession, the international banking industry meets a world full of profitable possibility. Offshore banking has proven itself to be a consistent money-making venture—even through times of economic downturn. How can you dismiss an industry that, as a whole, pays a negative two percent in tax? In other words, while other industries pay an average tax of 50 percent, offshore banks have had the federal government owing them money.

Consider that, in 1970, the Bank of America earned 19 percent of its total income offshore. By 1980, offshore profits accounted for a hefty 50 percent of its annual earnings. That same year, Citibank earned nearly 75 percent of its money offshore. The message is clear: major banks and corporations are involved in offshore banking because it makes money. Their leadership role should serve as a signal to smaller companies, investment consortiums, and individual entrepreneurs: offshore banking makes good, sound, profitable sense.

Customer Profit

Profit, like so many other offshore banking benefits, must be understood from two distinct vantage points: customer and owner. For discreet clients, foreign banking implies a level of earning power that could never be matched within the domestic banking system. Onshore financial institutions want your business and, to some extent, need it. But their public profile and legal status as U.S. banks have been long-established. Gaining several new customers or losing a few old ones will have little effect on their operations. Offshore banks, on the other hand, view customers as a precious and absolute commodity.

If you are contemplating an offshore bank account, know that every foreign financial institution—no matter its size or jurisdiction—must provide various financial services in order to maintain its legal status as a bank. In other words, small banks throughout the Caribbean and Pacific islands need your business, and they will go out of their way to get it. In the same way that specialized boutiques cater to their select clientele, offshore centers and their offshore banks try to ensure that their customers stay happy. That means they will provide you with more profit-making services in one year than an onshore bank could deliver in ten.

High Interest Rates

Essentially, there are five different ways in which customers can profit from offshore banking. And without question the most widely known is high interest. What is sometimes less publicized is the variety of interest-bearing services available. Let's review them:

- *Savings/deposit accounts* can be maintained for years or for just a day. Normally, the longer you keep your money on deposit, the more interest you earn. I know of one private offshore bank located in St. Vincent, where customers earn 14-percent-per-annum interest on funds held for nine years. But determine the kind of return you really want: slow, steady, long-term growth; regular and consistent income; or fast, short-term profit. Investigate jurisdictional options and bank choices before you make a final choice. Keep in mind that deposit accounts pay different rates of interest, depending on the currency involved. Stronger currencies yield lower interest than weak currencies.

- *Twin accounts* offer some clients a much-sought-after banking convenience. They combine a "current" (checking-type) account with a high-interest deposit account. The bulk of the client's money stays on hand in a high-interest deposit but a small balance is held on current account for everyday withdrawal. In the event the client finds himself awkwardly overdrawn, his bank simply transfers money from the deposit account to cover the difference.

- *Fiduciary accounts* are another way of earning interest profit. The Swiss in particular utilize this banking service. With a fiduciary account, you can actually earn money by using your offshore bank as a proxy investor. For instance, let's say you maintain a savings account in an offshore Swiss bank. You can direct your banker to invest all or part of your holdings in U.S. dollars and West German marks. The dollars will be purchased in New York and held (in the Swiss bank's account) in a U.S. bank. The deutschemarks will be held in a German bank in Frankfurt. For the record, it appears as though your Swiss bank is acting on its own behalf. Nonetheless, all profits earned on the currency exchange and any interest earned on the deposit are paid to you. The Swiss bank makes a small commission for the fiduciary service, and you make tax-free money because all profits were earned abroad.

- *High-interest certificate-of-deposit accounts* are another way investors can earn impressive interest. These CDs usually take the form of bearer certificates of deposit that can be freely traded or negotiated without the need to record any names. Such banking services—which yield high interest earnings and offer financial privacy—are not permitted in the United States.

Float Time

But offshore banking offers much more than interest earnings. Float time is, for many offshore users, an important extra. Let's consider the American Express company. Every day, people around the world exchange their cash for insured American Express Travelers Cheques. Literally millions of dollars are cycled through this process week after week. That money is not allowed to wait idly for months while vagabond vacationers cash one $50 check at a time. It is intelligently invested into high-interest T-bills and money-market accounts. In other words, during the time between purchase of insured checks and actual onshore bank clearing, American Express is earning interest on your money. That is called profit from the float.

As an individual offshore customer, you can profit from float time in a similar way. If you establish an interest-bearing checking account in a foreign jurisdiction, you can use it to pay your domestic bills. Then, when checks are deposited by your creditors, they begin a long trek back to your offshore bank for clearing. You can ordinarily expect the entire process to take between 30 and 40 days. And during that time, you will be earning interest on the money you maintain in the account.

Merchant Banking

I have referred to this banking convenience many times,

but without ever labeling it by name. Merchant banking is perhaps the most creative way to approach offshore profit potential. The Glass Spiegel Act effectively prohibits U.S. banks from engaging in the securities and brokerage businesses or investment counsel. Offshore banks are not bound by these restrictions. As a result, they are able to meet a comparatively wide range of your banking needs. Through the use of merchant banking, you can develop a comfortable financial rapport with just one banker who will provide you with investment counsel and discretionary-portfolio-investment management. With your approval he can make investments in whatever opportunity may offer a profitable return with acceptable risk.

Asset Protection

Another of offshore banking's profitable advantages is asset protection. The money you keep in domestic accounts is vulnerable to innumerable rules and regulations. Assets can be seized or frozen by the signature of just one court official. Very few situations short of murder would jeopardize the security of your offshore assets. So, the profit you earn is the money you keep. One of my clients came to appreciate this aspect of offshore banking when he found himself steeped in a long and complicated divorce case. Fortunately he had managed to spread his assets throughout the world. And, by establishing his own offshore bank in the Mariana Islands, he was insured against a community split on money earned outside the United States.

A "Hidden" Profit

Finally, offshore customers earn a kind of "hidden" profit. Because U.S. banks are legally required to maintain reserve assets that cannot be invested, they are very expensive to operate. In essence, domestic banks are unable to offer you a competitive interest rate because a sizable percentage of their funds remain tied up in profitless reserves. To help relieve some of that burden, onshore institutions routinely pass along to their customers a number of costly service charges. Again, because offshore banks are not confined in this way, they operate more efficiently. And you save money.

Owners and Profit

In almost every instance, offshore bank owners function as their own customers and concomitantly profit from the same benefits. But over and above these earnings, offshore bank owners reap impressive profits that are unavailable to the general public. Offshore banks make money in the same way onshore banks do: they borrow money at a low rate and then lend it at a higher rate.

All banks—foreign and domestic—borrow money from their depositors. For example, when you open a checking account at any commercial bank, you are really loaning the bank your money in exchange for the privilege of having a checkbook. Banks currently pay about 5-percent interest on checking accounts, enabling you to earn 5-percent interest on your money and necessitating that the bank earn at least 5-percent profit on the initial deposit if it is to break even. Needless to say, the bank's goal is to do better than that. So it takes your money, loans it out to third parties at nothing less than the prime lending rate, and keeps the difference as profit. An offshore bank works in the same way. Deposits are accepted and loans are made.

Taking Deposits

Locating potential deposits (and then wining, dining, and securing them) constitutes one of offshore banking's most intriguing activities. Be prepared for some uneasy moments in the beginning and anticipate some amusing capers as you grow more comfortable with the process. Basically, there are just three ways to garner funds, but the subtleties of each can keep you young or make you old, depending upon your ability to relax and enjoy the financial dynamics.

- I suspect that the most tried-and-true method of finding reputable depositors is non-U.S. advertising. Remember, you cannot advertise your bank or its services in domestic media because of certain provisions in onshore-banking law. You can, however, accept deposits from the American public, so long as you have reached them through non-U.S.-distributed publications such as the *International Herald Tribune* or the Latin American edition of *Time* magazine. Generally, those people who respond to these announcements are looking for a viable way to increase their assets. Your ad will inform them of the services you offer: the rate of interest you pay on various accounts, insurance policies available through your bank, the chances for responsible investment consultation, and other banking opportunities relevant to their needs. My experience has been that response to these non-U.S. publications often comes from people living in this country. At the same time, I have never run an ad without receiving at least a few foreign letters of query.

- Euromarket placement is a second way to solicit deposits. The Bank of England reported at the end of March, 1981, that its Eurocurrency deposits totaled $485 billion. A significant portion of those deposits were held in negotiable certificates of deposit issued by offshore banks.

The Eurocurrency market is simply money on deposit and available for lending at financial establishments outside the country of its origin. For example, dollars on deposit at banks outside the United States are considered Eurocurrency. So are deutschemarks deposited outside of West Germany. "Eurodollars" is the term for that portion of Eurocurrency deposits denominated in dollars. "Asia dollars" and "Latin dollars" are essentially the same as Eurodollars, except that they trade in Asia or Latin America rather than in Europe. The term "petrodollar," however, has a slightly different meaning. Petrodollars are those that arise from the sale of oil by oil-producing countries. They are usually transferred to the Eurodollar market and, in many cases, invested in certificates of deposit issued by offshore banks.

Since the Eurodollar market is largely unregulated, it is governed by competitive forces that are global in nature. The same dollars are funneled again and again between banks all over the world. This cycle of exchange constantly expands the market and benefits the international banking community—offshore institutions in particular. Why? Because transfer activity is reflected as an increase in business and thus as an increase in profits. And profit is the major goal of any offshore bank.

If an offshore bank is owned by a financially sound corporation or by a solvent private investor, it may be able to tap into the Eurodollar market. If so, it can place its own bank's certificates of deposit directly into the marketplace without undue effort or sales expense.

There are only two types of certificates of deposit that may be placed in the Eurodollar market. The first are referred to as "tap" CDs. They are issued to one broker or investor for a particular purpose, and vary a great deal in maturity, interest rate, amount, denomination of currency, and negotiability. But "tranche" CDs are far more common. They operate like bonds, are issued for a relatively large amount of money (i.e., $100,000, $200,000 or more), and are sliced into several pieces of perhaps $5,000 or $10,000. These slices are sold to the public, in bearer form, through market makers or brokers in the Eurodollar market. Because they are publicly held and negotiable, they are frequently advertised in international finance publications and in various European brokerage houses. Tranche CDs enjoy a large secondary market that enhances their liquidity and results in free trading among informed investors.

By applying Eurodollar-market techniques to the issuance of tranche CDs, offshore banks can sometimes utilize bearer certificates of deposit as a means to raise capital from among members of their financial consortium or from existing clients. And funds derived from the sale of these CDs may be loaned back to the bank's parent shareholders.

- There is one other way to secure deposits, and it involves private solicitation. Despite the fact that it can prove to be the most effective technique of all, private solicitation is best left to the seasoned offshore banker who feels confident with financial rhetoric and at ease among affluent investors. To legally solicit depositors within the United States, you must be certain that you make no public offering. In other words, if an impartial associate, employee, or acquaintance personally invites someone to open an account with your offshore bank, you will have no problem because, according to U.S. regulation, the potential depositor will have been approached through private solicitation.

In less than twenty-five years, offshore banks have successfully attracted thousands of investors worldwide. And their most persuasive selling tool has always been profit. As potential depositors examine their investment options, offshore banking grows more and more appealing. Where else can bank customers earn as high as 19- to 21-percent-per-annum interest on deposits?

Extending Credit

Once an offshore bank has acquired sufficient deposits, it can begin extending credit. The repetitive cycle of first obtaining and then loaning money constitutes the essence of all banking profit. Put simply, financial institutions make money only when they borrow low and lend high. But just as there are several ways of garnering deposits, there are a variety of methods of extending credit.

Letters of credit and financial guarantees are common forms of offshore credit. Both of them are detailed financial statements formalizing the conditions of a bank loan. The process typically begins with a letter of commitment from the bank. It explains to a prospective borrower that if he deposits a fixed sum of money for a specified period of time (usually ten years), the interest will be paid into a "sinking fund." This fund will, in turn, enable the bank to issue a letter of credit and financial guarantee for the amount of the deposit plus interest.

The offshore bank profits in three ways: it charges a nominal fee to issue the letter of commitment; it charges several percentage points to actually issue the loan guarantee; and it gains the use of its client's secured deposit during the period of time the guarantee is pending. If the borrower does not have enough capital to make the initial deposit, his offshore bank may loan him the money—in a separate arrangement and at a higher rate of interest than it pays to establish the sinking fund. Or, if the loan is obtained from a third party, the bank can charge an additional handling fee.

Back-to-back loans provide another method of extending credit. In a back-to-back loan, funds deposited by one corporate subsidiary can serve as the collateral for a loan extended to another subsidiary of the same parent company. In practice, this process of reciprocal lending and borrowing allows a diversified corporation to transfer its profits from a nation with a relatively high tax to a lower tax jurisdiction. For example, let's say that Transnational Machine Industries (TMI) is a diversified U.S. conglomerate with worldwide operations. Among its many financial activities is a privately held offshore bank in Montserrat called the Overseas Security Bank. Via its own offshore bank facility, TMI can deposit profits from its U.S. divisions and loan that money to its divisions in Hong Kong. By utilizing a back-to-back loan, TMI escapes a 50-percent U.S. tax on profits and replaces it with Hong Kong's substantially lower tax rate.

Secured lending is still another way of extending credit. Nearly all offshore banks take advantage of opportunities to loan money. Their most frequently issued loans involve venture capital—in other words, high-risk loans at high interest rates. The profits earned from secured lending may be 5 to 10 percentage points higher than on loans made by conventional lenders.

Within the United States, strict laws govern the tendering of money at excessively high interest rates. Domestic banks must follow the letter of those laws in every case. But a 1977 California court case tested the extent to which U.S. regulation could determine the lending activities of foreign banking corporations. In *Sondeno v. Union Commerce Bank*, the Court held that offshore banking institutions were exempt from California usury laws.

Investing

But if an offshore banker simply takes deposits and extends credit, he will certainly have missed the core of real profit potential. The legends that surround offshore banking and its impressive money-making possibilities are the result of wise investment. To begin with, deposits are considered liabilities on a bank's financial statement. Offshore banks make money not because they are able to garner international funds, but because once those funds are safely deposited, the bank invests them in high-yielding ventures. Intelligent investments invariably earn the bank more money than it is required to pay out to its depositors—no matter what rate of interest it boasts. This earning power is possible because offshore banks are not bound by the investment restrictions that bind onshore banks. Instead, they are at liberty to invest in any number of opportunities—from real estate and high-ticket consumer goods to securities. Literally anything within the wide parameters of international investment is open to an offshore-bank owner. It is my opinion that even if you were to factor out all other money-making capabilities, the single freedom to creatively invest in profitable ventures would be reason enough to become involved in offshore banking.

Taking deposits, extending credit, and making investments—these are the three big ways to earn offshore profit. None of the activities can effectively function without the other two. But working together they constitute offshore banking's profit triad. It's a powerful combination.

Bonus Profits

Aside from the profit triad laid out above, your own offshore bank will earn several bonus profits. All of them are predicated on the fact that offshore banks provide services well beyond the scope of onshore banks. As an offshore bank owner, you are free to capitalize on any of the following nine benefits:

Check Float

I read an article in *Business Week* a few years ago called "Making Millions by Stretching the Float." See how you react to the profit potential discussed.

"For the past four years, Houston-based Exxon Co., U.S.A., the giant domestic subsidiary of Exxon Corp., has been using the disbursement-float notion to some degree on the $5 million to $6 million it averages each day in cash payments. The idea works this way:

"Say that Exxon pays a supplier in Dallas $1 million with a check drawn on a central account in Houston. Once the supplier deposits the check, as few as two days may elapse before the check is presented for payment to Exxon's Houston bank.

"But if Exxon pays that Dallas supplier the $1 million with a check drawn on a special remote disbursing account' in a small branch of a major regional bank in, say, North Carolina, the check is forced through at least two Federal Reserve Banks, and the float can be extended to as much as five days.

"By special arrangement with the North Carolina bank, Exxon can delay funding the disbursement account until the day after the check is presented for collection. Counting mailing time, the time required for the check to be processed through the supplier's books and deposited, and the time the check is floating through the Fed's clearing system, Exxon can hold onto its $1 million in cash for as long as two weeks after it issues the check and thus keep earning interest on the funds.

"Exxon, in fact, uses such accounts in North Carolina to pay suppliers west of the Mississippi, and other accounts in Arizona (which has no regional Federal Reserve bank) to pay suppliers on the East Coast. Bankers figure that such an arrangement can enable a company to keep an average of 1 percent of its total disbursements at work earning extra interest. In the case of a large corporation paying out $5 million a day, the concept can allow it to hold onto an additional $12 million in cash during the year, adding more than $1 million a year to its pretax income at present interest levels."

—*Business Week*, 1974

Imagine what could be done if that central disbursement account were offshore. One of my clients established his private St. Vincent bank for precisely this reason. Jack has been exceptionally successful in taking advantage of the check-float time between his dry-cleaning businesses in the United States and his St. Vincent checking account. Island Security Bank makes it feasible for Jack to issue checks for goods and services with the knowledge that he has from thirty to forty days before they will clear his offshore bank. In the meantime, he earns tax-free interest on the money in the account. Last year, Jack probably made close to $40,000 in check-float profit—more than enough money to establish still another offshore bank in some other jurisdiction.

Currency Exchange

Many offshore banks take advantage of their opportunity to exchange currency. The service is usually extended to residents of foreign countries, where currency cannot be converted. For instance, offshore facilities often work in association with South African clients wanting to convert their national currency into U.S. dollars. The transaction is absolutely legal because offshore banks are immune to local currency exchange restrictions.

Certainly, the bank profits: it earns a handsome commission (sometimes as high as 20 percent of the deposit) to accommodate the special drawing request.

Commodities Brokerage

I know of another privately owned offshore bank (this one

located in the Cayman Islands) that earns sizable profit through commodities brokerage. In one transaction, the U.S. bank owner made in excess of $400,000—simply by making appropriate business decisions and then moving papers back and forth. The Island Security Bank is held privately by a Miami businessman who acts as its Special North American Advisor. In this case, he was able to purchase several hundred thousand pounds of coffee by issuing his own letter of credit to a Columbian seller. The terms specified that delivery would be made to one of the bank's clients, named at a later date. While the Miami bank owner had the coffee tied up with his letter of credit, he found a European buyer and negotiated a profitable sale. In just six weeks, the Cayman bank processed the entire transaction without risk.

Providing Insurance

Some offshore financial centers permit their nonresident banks to operate as insurance companies. In these foreign jurisdictions, bank owners can underwrite and insure risks. Moreover, premiums paid to the bank are fully deductible in most cases. The ability to profit substantially from insurance services depends on marketplace competition and upon the relative cost of similar insurance within the United States. When they work best, captive insurance services include any number of high-risk concerns—from malpractice or strike insurance to coverage that would be outrageously expensive or downright impossible to obtain through a domestic carrier. There are at least two offshore banks on the island of St. Vincent offering their clients life, casualty, auto, theft, and fire coverage. For high-risk U.S. residents, the service is a major incentive to move assets out of their domestic banks and into St. Vincent. Both banks earn their profit from annual premiums that are high, but not as high as comparable coverage purchased here in the States.

Secret Numbered Accounts

According to some financial experts, secret numbered accounts are more trouble than they are worth. Undeniably, they involve a lot of time and an initial expenditure of money because they must be opened in person. Nonetheless, I tend to agree with privacy expert Mark Skousen when he says that "they do serve their purpose under unusual circumstances. A spy might be paid directly through a numbered account. . . . A Latin American businessman might have an anonymous account as insurance against a coup d'etat. A Soviet dissident writer might have money from book royalties stashed away in a secret bank account, waiting for the time when he will be allowed to emigrate. And there may come a time when unpopular political figures in the United States will seek financial asylum through a Swiss numbered account. The disadvantages must be weighed, but the benefits may someday exceed the costs."

Not all offshore banking centers offer the Swiss-style numbered bank account. So, if you are interested in complete anonymity (or feel that your assets will be safe only so long as your identity is kept confidential), be sure to ask prospective bankers if they provide the service. If you decide to establish your own offshore facility, think about choosing a locale that allows you to offer secret numbered accounts. You'll be able to attract an entire community of international customers. Swiss banks usually charge negative interest to provide the service, but if you extend the courtesy free of charge, you will stand to garner disgruntled European clients.

Trusts

Most offshore banks find it profitable to provide trust-company services. Acting as trustee under deeds of settlement or will, receiving assets on behalf of clients, and managing, administering, and investing them in accordance with their instructions can prove a lucrative offshore service. I know that some offshore banks charge up to $10,000 to administer any given trust.

Cash Management

Whether we're talking about an individual or a company, cash management suggests the best possible utilization of dormant cash. The main objective for any banker is to ensure that his bank's capital is legally invested and utilized in the highest yielding opportunity. His ability to make the right financial decisions at the right time will determine his bank's profit, his clients' profit, and his own professional reputation. Naturally, all banks (irrespective of their location) would like to invest their long-term deposits into high-yielding ventures such as commodities or real estate. Unfortunately, U.S. facilities are prohibited from doing so by onshore banking laws. Offshore banks are far less constrained. They can legally invest all of their capital—long- or short-term—in any investment opportunity they choose. In fact, it is for just this reason that many domestic banks eventually establish an offshore subsidiary facility: to make investments that would be prohibited here at home.

Arbitrage Opportunity

"Arbitrage" generally means the simultaneous buying and selling of the same (or equivalent) securities in different markets. When an offshore bank carefully takes advantage of the arbitrage process, it capitalizes on important marketplace variables. In the foreign money market, currency values fluctuate from one market to another. An astute offshore banker (or financial representative) monitors various currency values in a number of different markets. A careful eye and good intuition allow him to buy low and sell high— all in the same moment. And he can keep the difference as bank profit. When the value "spread" is there and the opportunity is perceived, cross trades can be completed within a matter of minutes.

For example, an offshore bank (through its foreign exchange trader in London) buys deutschemarks for its account in Frankfurt and immediately sells them for Italian lire. But that is just step one. If the offshore trader can locate a broker— perhaps in Zurich—who needs lire, he can trade again, this time for many more deutschemarks than he started with. Even after deducting telephone and telex expenses, the offshore bank is likely to finish with an impressive profit. And all for a fast, risk-free paper transaction.

Interest-rate arbitrage is a far more common source of off-shore bank profit. It normally involves converting funds from one market to another for the purpose of investing and obtaining a higher rate of interest than would otherwise be available. Sometimes, it involves moving money abroad through the exchange market so it will be available at a lower interest rate. The offshore bank stands to earn a handsome profit from the process. First, because it receives a more favorable brokerage rate for the purchase and sale of funds. Second, because all resulting profits are technically considered bank profits that may be maintained tax-free. And finally, because the service attracts customers who might otherwise do business elsewhere.

Bank-to-Bank Loans

Offshore banks earn a sort of bonus profit when they deal with one another. Quite possibly you have heard of LIBOR, the London Interbank Lending Rate, the special interest rate at which banks borrow money from each other. An offshore bank typically borrows at LIBOR and, in turn, loans the money to third parties at a considerably higher interest rate. The spread between LIBOR and the bank's prime lending rate constitutes the facility's profit.

Minimizing Costs

Don't overlook the obvious. Offshore banks earn a fair share of their total "profit" because they are uniquely able to minimize the cost of doing business. Put simply: what they do not spend to operate, they keep as profit. Their ability to borrow funds at below prime interest, their exceptional opportunity to save on transaction fees, and their change to offer exciting investment banking services without exorbitant operating costs such as the maintenance of reserves all amount to money saved. That savings equals new profit.

So whether you approach offshore profit from the perspective of an aggressive businessman or a passive investor, you inevitably find an expanded universe of money-making opportunity. By establishing and operating your own offshore facility, you can take deposits and invest them wisely, loan money and earn on interest, conduct trust activity, capitalize on check-float time, or hire a trained management consultant to handle all the work for you. You can run and star in the show yourself, or opt to stand on the sidelines—counting your money!

CHAPTER 5

PRIVACY

Personal privacy is something we all take for granted. Too often, the right to conduct our lives in confidentiality becomes important only after we learn what it might be like to live without the option. In my opinion, that's what happened to an old friend of mine.

Steve went on to medical school after he finished his undergraduate work. I heard later that he'd married the girl he had been going with since his sophomore year. Evidently, he had done pretty well because when I saw him in 1979, he had already established a respected Beverly Hills practice, purchased two homes and a summer cabin at Lake Tahoe, was driving a luxury automobile, and was thinking about the possibility of opening a small boutique for his wife's design line.

I remember being impressed by his uncanny instincts for the right investments. In just a few years, he had managed to amass a small fortune, following all the established rules, diversifying his assets in real estate, stocks and bonds, funds, money-market accounts, and even a few high-risk business ventures. Unfortunately, he had kept all his assets onshore. That error cost him a great deal.

Nearly three years went by before I ran into him again. Although he didn't give me all the details, he did say he had been through an ugly divorce. The scenario sounded relatively familiar. His wife had hired a private detective to uncover any clandestine activities that might be used against him in court. When she learned about an ongoing affair he was having, she filed for divorce and sued him for half of everything he owned. He had also been sued for malpractice, costing him months of professional agony and thousands of dollars in legal fees.

Between the two court cases and attendant media coverage, enough information was revealed about his personal and financial activities that the IRS moved in for an extensive audit. After all the settlements were completed and the losses accounted for, Steve moved to another state and was in the midst of starting all over again. As he said, he had planned for everything—except contingencies. So, when things got really tough, he had no way of protecting his personal privacy or his financial investments. Once in court, everything became an open book. And everyone took advantage of his position.

Needless to say, offshore banking would not have solved all of Steve's problems. It could not have saved his marriage, or prevented the malpractice suit, or even the IRS audit. But it could have protected him from the extensive invasion of his financial privacy. Had a fair share of his assets been held offshore, Steve might have been able to legally avoid paying enormous sums of money to a furious wife, a bureaucratic legal system, and the Internal Revenue Service.

Your privacy is invaded every day. Without even realizing it, you allow the government, your banks, and other powerful institutions to collect information about your personal and professional life. Recent reports indicate that there are some fifty files kept on each and every one of us. Among them are motor-vehicle licenses and registrations; professional licenses; Social Security files; federal, state, and local tax returns; school records; birth, marriage, and death certificates; military and veterans records; FBI and police records; court documents; deeds; passports; and census forms.

For people operating their own businesses, there is a second complete set of data maintained and updated on a regular basis: insurance-company records, employment-agency files, bank and financial-institution records, as well as brokerage-house and other investment reports. Ironically, the experts agree that we ourselves provide these institutions with the bulk of their information. In fact, one study has revealed that more than 72 percent of the time, data sources obtain their information from the very people they are monitoring.

Financial transactions in particular are coming under careful scrutiny. Every time you cash a check, apply for credit, purchase an insurance policy, seek employment, or attempt to enter a facility with controlled access, you are asked to provide information regarding your personal money matters. Annual income-tax filings and other financial reporting requirements collect additional data, and you are that much more susceptible to intrusive probes by outside sources.

All of this can make you feel a bit paranoid. But there are legitimate reasons for suspicion. Did you know, for instance, that:

- The U.S. Treasury Department keeps in computer memory the names and addresses of all Americans who maintain foreign bank accounts.

- Several new technologies allow private investigators and government agencies to eavesdrop on telephone lines without detection.

- The Passport Office may soon begin issuing a "machine-readable" passport that will be used to monitor airline reservations, financial transactions, and all your movements into and out of the country.

- The Supreme Court has ruled that evidence obtained illegally by the IRS can be used to convict a taxpayer—a decision that will encourage future covert action and government misconduct against "suspected citizens."

The logical solution, of course, is to keep silent about all your personal and financial affairs. But that is far easier said than done, especially when the questions come from a government that has authority over much of your life. As the federal bureaucracy tightens its grip on the movement of money—within the country and outside of it—your personal privacy withers. In fact when we look at today's economic surveillance and accelerating technological developments, George Orwell's 1984 seems closer than ever.

The Writing on the Wall

In general, I have found that financial privacy is a relative priority. Like religion, romance, political affiliations, and even beauty, privacy means little to some people but everything to others. I work with a few clients who place surprisingly little importance on closed-door banking. Others refuse to enter into any business venture without a firm commitment that all transactions will remain confidential. If you're a privacy-concerned investor, offshore banking can offer you one of today's most confidential financial environments.

Just to test your own priorities, how do you react to the expanding implementation of "check truncation"? Once put into practice at your local bank, this new system will render your canceled checks and monthly balance sheets a thing of the past. Every few weeks, you will receive a single computer readout detailing your checking expenditures—when you wrote a check, to whom, and for how much. And your bank will store that information in its computers, where it can be easily retrieved for reference for monitoring purposes. Without exaggeration, check truncation will allow your bank to compile a detailed dossier of your entire checking account.

How much does your checking account tell about you? Just go through your checks for the past few months and see for yourself. They show where you live, shop, eat, and travel; what political organizations you support, and what recreational activities you enjoy. They give a pretty clear picture of where your children go to college, what sort of friends you have, and even who your relatives are. Through check truncation, all this personal information will be available to strangers.

Perhaps you feel completely comfortable with this information and are willing to see it disclosed. That's certainly your right. The issue, however, concerns the rights of those Americans who do not want such details available to anyone for the asking. How can their rights to privacy be protected? Although relatively few domestic banks have begun working with check truncation, it is expected that by 1990 nearly all will have instituted the practice. When that time comes, what can bank customers do to maintain their financial privacy?

Consider, too, the paradox of a federal government— theoretically responsible for protecting your privacy—that has become a principal informant in the story of dwindling financial freedom. According to a 1982 report in the *Los Angeles Times*, "More . . . companies are getting from the government things that people thought were confidential. Thanks to the computer . . . government records are no longer inaccessible old files, hard to reach and harder to copy. Now the data is 'manipulable'—easily compiled, easily stored, and very easily and selectively extracted."

The mistake we often make is to assume that federal law protects our privacy. It does not. The *Times* report went on to say that "the consumer is on his own in the effort to control exploitation of his name. Despite recently enacted privacy laws, and despite a growing popular movement to protect 'data privacy,' the personal details of a citizen's life do not get much protection from lawmakers. California law, for instance, even defines names, addresses, and phone numbers as nonpersonal information.' "

Sophisticated technology also conspires against the privacy-concerned individual. The truth is that computers are now talking to one another with an ease and frequency unimagined just a decade ago. The data stored in the memory banks of these machines is accessible information, on file for people, government agencies, and private security firms via remote computer terminals and telephone lines.

High-school computer whiz kids have demonstrated an extraordinary ability to break into computer systems and access classified information. If they can do it, think of what the IRS can do when it decides to pursue a taxpayer. And consider the financial havoc that can be wrought by a determined and sophisticated collection agency intent on getting its money. Anyone with a $300 computer terminal and basic programming ability can become an electronic Sherlock Holmes.

The danger is not imagined. It is all too real. Although there is no foolproof way to ensure that personal information about you remains confidential, there are ways to stay fairly protected from undue intrusion. Remember, financial privacy demands that you minimize the amount of information created about you and limit access to the information that already exists. Voila! Offshore banking.

Background on Financial Privacy

I do not want to present offshore banking as the solution to futuristic frenzy. Nor do I wish to shake a naive finger at high technology. Technological expertise is not the culprit. It is the challenge—to be confronted by men and women of conscious intent. Unfortunately, when it comes to issues of privacy, technology often seems to be manipulated and thrust into a spiral of intrusive sophistication. But even when you look beyond these modern developments, you see a long-established, historical rationale for maintaining financial privacy.

Discrimination

Throughout the centuries, different peoples have found themselves persecuted because of race, religion, or political beliefs. At various times, in various places, Jews, blacks, Asians, Protestants, Catholics, and many others have known the pain of discrimination. Sometimes it has meant the blatant confiscation of property, imprisonment, even death.

Recent history is full of examples of people forced to leave their homes or nations of origin without notice. Hundreds of Asians were expelled from Uganda by Idi Amin. They, of course, were not allowed to take assets and other property along with them. Millions of Jews in Germany lost everything. And even here, in our own country, Japanese Americans found themselves incarcerated in concentration camps during World War II. To this day, no reparations have been paid for their substantial economic losses.

Look at your own life. Although the U.S. still affords the greatest freedoms in the world, it cannot be anything less than wise to keep a little nestegg—some money and a few assets— beyond the reach of those who might one day try to conquer.

Offshore banking can afford you that luxury, and allow for substantial benefits along the way.

Excessive Government

Unfortunately, governments sometimes have a real interest in the persecution of certain political, religious, or racial groups. Pilgrims left England to escape religious discrimination. American colonists later revolted against the British government due to unreasonable taxation.

In times of crisis, governments often persecute the financially independent by means of price controls, rationing, foreign-exchange controls, prohibition of foreign accounts, confiscation of property, and high taxes. War, even the threat of war, can carry with it a string of government restrictions. During difficult times, governments will go to any lengths to control certain people's lives. And, more often than not, the majority supports such action.

For example, throughout World War II, virtually every country engaged in some form of economic sanction. The U.S. government froze all German and subsequently Swiss assets within this country. Later, during the 1956 Suez crisis, Egyptian accounts were blocked by American and British banks. As recently as 1980, President Carter froze all Iranian assets in the United States. And, during the 1982 Falklands crisis, our government imposed strict economic sanctions against Argentina.

Smart investors living in politically vulnerable countries often keep the bulk of their money offshore. Often, they establish their own foreign banks. Sometimes, they simply hide their money in secret caches. Overriding fears of government restriction and expropriation have pushed them into a no-choice position. As Americans, we are far less fearful. But even here, a growing concern centers on government intransigence regarding people's economic liberty. An additional concern preoccupies many European investors, who worry about the possibility of a Soviet or Eurocommunist takeover. As a result, quiet transfers of money and assets have become common between Western European countries and the United States.

Different countries utilize different techniques to monitor and thereby control the financial activities of their citizens. But by and large, three distinct methods define the governmental challenge:

Currency Control. During war (and even through times of peace), governments seem to enjoy implementing foreign-exchange controls. In fact, just twenty countries in the entire world now allow for total exchange freedom.

Fortunately, the United States is one of them. But that may change. A number of recent developments point to an increasing federal concern over the movement of money—within the country and, most especially, outside of it. For instance, under the Bank Secrecy Act of 1970, citizens are legally required to report all transfers of money across the border that exceed $5,000. You must also acknowledge the existence of any foreign bank accounts when completing your annual tax return. For their part, banks must keep records of all checks over $10,000 that are sent abroad. Many experts see these regulations as the forerunners of more restrictive exchange control and less financial privacy.

War Against Gold. For more than forty years, the United States had laws forbidding citizens to own gold. In 1975, however, those laws were nullified. Today, Americans are free to legally own and trade gold without government restriction. But what about tomorrow? Or next year? We have no way of knowing whether the government may again outlaw gold ownership. If it ever does, people may be forced to turn in their gold assets at well below a fair market price.

In his recent book *Guide to Financial Privacy*, Mark Skousen says that the federal government never really stopped its attack on "hard money." He calls the recent ban against holding collectibles (such as gold and silver coins) in self-directed retirement programs "ill-conceived legislation" which was "incorporated at the last moment into Reagan's 1981 tax bill by lobbyists for the banks and other antigold forces who want to deny an important 'alternative investment' to the U.S. investor." Even more important, he explains that "this amendment to the tax bill gives unlimited power to the Secretary of the Treasury to forbid other pension investments it deems 'unsound' or otherwise unfavorable at its own discretion!"

Antigold measures also include a number of Congressional bills which, if passed, would eliminate the long-term capital-gains tax benefits on gold, silver, and other collectibles. While such legislation has little chance of passing today, it could very well pass in the near future. Consider the fact that in France all buyers and sellers of gold coins are required to register their transactions with the federal government. Many people have begun to wonder how long it will be before the United States demands similar registration.

Confiscatory Taxes. I have yet to meet a man or woman who enjoys paying taxes. Whether your income implies a small tax load or an enormous one, it is frustrating to think about mandatory "contributions" to Uncle Sam.

In this country, we have what is termed a "progressive tax structure" that imposes the heaviest tax load on the highest income earners. In virtually every state—from California to Massachusetts—citizens are protesting its effects. Tallied votes have made it quite clear that people resent property taxes and bond issues. Perhaps even more revealing is the startling growth of America's "underground economy." As taxes get higher, more and more people are transacting business off the record. One academic researcher estimates that hundreds of billions of dollars' worth of income go unreported every year. Unless some action is taken soon, the vast majority of taxpayers will be underreporting their annual incomes just to economically survive. I am not advocating that you become part of this underground economy, but I would suggest that you maintain as much financial privacy as possible. By keeping business transactions confidential, you can legally minimize your tax load.

Gossip and False Information

Have you ever been the target of ugly gossip or intentional misinformation? Celebrities sometimes sue for such intrusion on their privacy. Less notable individuals are too often unable to take that option.

James Millstone, an assistant managing editor of the *St. Louis Post-Dispatch*, found himself in just such a predicament. When a routine credit check turned up some damaging information, no one thought to verify the facts. It seems an angry neighbor reported that Millstone was a long-haired hippie who used drugs and abused his children. As a result, his credit rating was destroyed and his auto insurance company seriously considered canceling his policy. Millstone intelligently pushed to know the reason for the trouble, learned about the distorted credit report, and went to court. He was ultimately vindicated, but the entire episode cost him four years and several thousand dollars.

Even passing remarks made before neighbors, friends, or business acquaintances can invade your privacy and damage your reputation. For instance, doctors are sworn to professional confidentiality, but they are not always true to that oath. Recently, one physician reported to a prospective employer that her patient might have difficulty handling his money. The comment was hardly a medical judgment, yet it effectively kept someone from getting a job he deserved.

As you may know, the salaries of top executives are regularly published in national media. Not long ago, the *Wall Street Journal* ran an article examining this issue from the executives' perspective. The wife of one corporate president complained that because her husband's salary was published annually in the local paper, she and her children confronted resentment from their friends and neighbors.

There are many reasons why people keep their money matters private. For some, there is the possible embarrassment associated with past mistakes. Bankruptcy, draft evasion, or a criminal record may be a part of your personal history that you would prefer to keep private. The truth is that we do not live in a perfect world. People do not dismiss the past and they are not willing to judge associates only on the grounds of firsthand experience. If, for whatever reason, you are anxious to separate your past from your present, financial privacy is imperative.

Lawsuits

As my friend Steve discovered too late, the threat of costly lawsuits is one of the most practical reasons for maintaining financial privacy. Countless fights have taken place in courtrooms the world over involving large sums of money and vengeful antagonists. The inclination to sue at the least provocation is on the verge of becoming an epidemic. And the likeliest targets are the people with the most money.

Theft

As society grows more complex, and as our urban problems intensify, crime increases. In so threatening an environment, it pays to downplay your financial success. For your own protection, try to maintain a low profile. Perhaps you should consider living in a less ostentatious home than you can actually afford, or driving an older car. Why make it obvious that you are a handsome target?

Aside from burglary and other forms of physical theft, it is a good idea to protect yourself against fraudulent investment schemes. Have you ever lost money investing in a managed commodity program? Or in some esoteric stock pushed on you by an overeager stockbroker? Perhaps you have fallen for the high-pressure telephone salesman who persuades you to buy precious metals on margin—only to later find yourself with several thousand dollars less money. Many seasoned as well as novice investors succumb to the apparently refined terminology of so-called investment "experts." More often than not, these charmers promise you the moon but give you green cheese. The only one who profits from the transaction is the expert, and you're left holding the empty bag.

Privacy and Big Government

It was not always so difficult to maintain privacy—financial or otherwise. In fact, our right to conduct personal affairs without outside intrusion was originally secured by the Bill of Rights. Our founding fathers came to this continent because their homelands had denied them the liberty to live as they saw fit. They were determined to plot a new political course for this country.

The First Amendment guarantees that "Congress shall make no law . . . abridging the freedom of speech, or of the press; or the right of the people peaceably to assemble, and to petition the Government for the redress of grievances." Certainly, that would ensure free communication between investors and their financial advisors and brokers. Whether the communication is conducted through the mail, over the telephone, or via individual intermediaries, U.S. citizens should be free to exchange information regarding the distribution and diversification of their assets. And if the federal government decides to check your mail or monitor your calls in order to collect information on your financial transactions, your First Amendment rights are in all probability being violated.

Nonetheless, the Securities and Exchange Commission (SEC) has restricted financial advice and communication for nearly fifty years. Based on the Investment Advisors Act of 1933, all financial advisors and investment newsletters must be registered with the SEC. Furthermore, the Commission specifies certain accounting procedures be utilized by all investors and their advisors. If business transactions are processed or monitored in any other way, both individuals may be found in violation of the law.

The Act also gives the SEC authority to legally enter an advisor's or publisher's office (without warning) for the sole purpose of inspecting accounts and mailing lists. It requires investment advisors to forewarn all clients that the purchase of unregistered foreign stocks carries certain legal risk. All of this violates the spirit of the First Amendment because it limits our right to freely communicate with whomever we please.

The Fourth Amendment is equally germane to any discussion of financial privacy. It specifies that "the right of the people to be secure in their persons, houses, papers, and effects against unreasonable searches and seizures shall not be violated and no warrants shall issue, but upon probable cause. . . ." I am constantly astounded by the government's determination to circumvent this Constitutional provision.

In 1970, Congress passed the Bank Secrecy Act, requiring all domestic banks to maintain duplicate records of their transactions. The central premise of the Act was that "an effective fight on crime depends, in large measure, on the maintenance of adequate and appropriate records by financial institutions." I don't suppose that the law was originally intended to unleash government fishing expeditions into the banking records of individual citizens. Nonetheless, that is what has happened. In fact, the U.S. Supreme Court ruled in *U.S. vs. Miller* that bank customers—whose records are sought by the government for whatever reason—have no right to ensure that access is controlled by an "existing legal process."

Since the Miller decision, things have changed again. In 1976, for instance, Congress passed the Tax Reform Act, allowing onshore bank customers to challenge the IRS in the event that the agency decided to seize bank records. But the law did not restore Fourth Amendment rights; it simply limited IRS authority in certain situations. If a law-enforcement agency other than the IRS sought bank records, citizens had no legal recourse.

Finally, in 1978, Congress passed the Financial Privacy Act. With this piece of legislation, the Miller decision was essentially overruled. Today, the federal government must notify you before—and give you the opportunity to challenge—any record search. Banks, savings-and-loan associations, and credit-card companies all fall under the wording of the Act.

Financial privacy is also a fundamental issue in the Fifth Amendment, which states that no citizen ". . . shall be com-

pelled in any criminal case to be witness against himself, nor
be deprived of life, liberty, or property, without due process
of law. . . ." No one should ever be required to incriminate
himself. Clearly, this is a relevant point in any tax-evasion
case. But it also has bearing in terms of alleged fraud and other
lawsuits. Unfortunately, the courts have narrowly defined
"private papers" as those held only by a bank customer, and
not by third parties.

In short, our most basic rights to privacy are systematically violated by a government that was originally designed to
protect its citizens from undue intrusion. Seen in this light,
the United States simply appears too risky an environment
for investors concerned with financial privacy. Why keep
assets within the country (and know that your banking transactions are monitored by the federal government), when you
can maintain those holdings—in privacy—offshore?

Offshore Banking: Privacy Insurance

Moving assets offshore to ensure financial privacy is not
a recent phenomenon. Perceptive investors have known for
some time that money could be more profitably managed and
better insulated from seizure in offshore jurisdictions. And for
their part, offshore officials have known for a long time that
international investors want banking privacy. In this vein, they
have competitively strengthened their regional secrecy laws
to accord offshore customers an impenetrable financial
sanctuary.

Needless to say, the federal government would like to cur-
tail the offshore-banking boom. After all, the money this country loses every year to foreign centers would help pay a healthy
chunk of our enormous annual deficit. Most recently, the
Reagan Administration has sought to intimidate certain offshore jurisdictions by reminding them that the U.S. government can, at any time, discontinue financial aid by terminating
its Caribbean economic development plan. The Bahamas, the
Caymans, Panama, and the Antilles are all being threatened
with the loss of annual subsidies should they fail to cooperate

with our federal tax investigations.

As pressure from the United States increases, offshore centers are growing more adept at circumventing complex red tape and international regulation. The island of St. Vincent is a good example of one such jurisdiction. In 1977, this small Caribbean government found a clever way to use its Official Secrecy Act to protect the confidentiality of local offshore bankers.

Island officials decided that their Trust Authority (which is simply a body of government) could, upon occasion, act as the resident agent of an offshore bank. They reasoned that if the Trust Authority were to act as the bank owner's island representative, then the Secrecy Act would apply, and the banker's priorities would be addressed. It works like this: St. Vincent's Official Secrecy Act makes it a criminal offense for any employee of the Trust Authority acting as a bank's resident representative to reveal information to third parties. So, if a U.S. government agent or private investigator goes to St. Vincent in an attempt to obtain financial information regarding one of the island's bank owners, he is told by the bank's local representative that no information may be given. And there are no exceptions.

Furthermore, U.S. tax liens and writs of execution are meaningless in St. Vincent. Because there is no covenant, agreement, or international treaty binding the island government to honor a foreign writ of execution, offshore bankers can rest assured that their assets are safe from all seizure.

Not every offshore center offers such extreme financial privacy. Countries vary a great deal in their commitment to confidentiality. But they are all acutely aware that they will successfully attract and maintain foreign capital only if they offer maximum banking secrecy. For instance, Switzerland was once considered the ultimate bastion of banking privacy. As a result, it was the world's most powerful international money center. But slowly the Swiss ethic and psychology shifted. The national emphasis on personal and financial privacy gave way to new priorities, and the country began losing investors to other, more welcoming locations.

Some people say that the beginning of the end came in 1977, when a Swiss-U.S. tax treaty went into effect. As investment advisor Gary North has said, "The once sacrosanct idea of banking secrecy is no longer sacrosanct in Switzerland. Bureaucrats and politicians in Switzerland are beginning to act like bureaucrats and politicians everywhere else. This is an ominous sign. Those who rest confidently on the tradition of Swiss banking secrecy may very well be resting on a weak reed—or worse yet, on a sword." There are many qualified experts who dispute North's pessimistic assessment. Yet, there can be no denying that the U.S. government is currently capable of applying persuasive pressure to Switzerland's banking community.

The lesson to be learned is fairly obvious: it can be dangerous to trust completely in any location's secrecy laws— no matter how airtight they may appear. However, in effect, they can provide you with the financial privacy you require. But laws change. They get overturned or overthrown. For this reason, investors seeking privacy protection should constantly monitor legal developments here and abroad. Make a habit of comparing various offshore jurisdictions. And move to transfer your assets before someone else moves to seize them.

Gaining Privacy Through Offshore Banks

Granted, U.S. enforcement agencies do appear most intent on collecting information about citizens' international business dealings. But to concentrate only on the ways in which an offshore bank cloaks assets from the federal government is to ignore its host of other privacy benefits. For American businessmen in particular, offshore banking offers myriad privacy protections. Let's review a few of them.

Aggressive Competition

One of the most important privacy benefits obtained from offshore banking is practical protection from overly aggressive competitors. Let's say you become involved in a business situation that ultimately leads to a lawsuit. If you bank within the United States, a court may award your competitor legal access to your financial records, and your position may be seriously jeopardized. If, on the other hand, your records are kept in an offshore bank, they are impervious to court orders.

Trade-Secret Protection

Another important privacy consideration involves the right to maintain healthy distance between creative ideas and outside encroachment. For instance, let's assume you have a formula or patent you want to protect. If you opt to copyright the idea in the United States, you must disclose it to the Copyright Office. In the process, your million-dollar concept becomes part of the public domain. Before you have time to establish a firm market, that concept can be reformulated— with only minor changes—and translated into your strongest competition.

Instead of going to the appropriate onshore office to file your formula, why not convert it into financial information? Call it "the exhibit to an agreement between a scientist and the formula's owner." If the formula's owner just so happens to be an offshore bank, the exhibit is likely to be protected under the bank secrecy laws of the relevant offshore jurisdiction.

Flight Capital

Certain countries are less stable than others. Ordinarily, the less stable the government, the more important it is to move assets offshore. For the person who wishes to move money out of a politically volatile environment, financial secrecy becomes more than a luxury. For this person it can mean the difference between freedom and imprisonment. In these cases, clients need to be assured that all bank transactions are cloaked in absolute secrecy. Offshore banking can make that promise. And keep it.

Privacy of Bank Records

If you had the proper credential and just $50, you could quite possibly gather the following information and material on any individual: checks (both front and back copies), bank statements, signature cards, loan applications, deposit and withdrawal slips, as well as all bank communications. And the poor devil would never know his private records had been obtained without approval.

Domestic banks typically release records in the event of civil litigation, criminal proceedings, an SEC investigation, and in any IRS audit. Private investigators often pose as officials with federal authority to review bank records. In this way, they are also privy to what you suppose is confidential information.

By utilizing an offshore bank, you ensure against any such invasion. And you can avoid the potentially troublesome requirement of having all your cash transactions (of more than $10,000) reported to the IRS. It can initially sound complex, but the legal principles creating this reporting loophole are quite straightforward.

Large transactions involving private individuals are, in all cases, duly recorded. But when two domestic banks transfer funds—for whatever reason—no reporting requirement is imposed. Recently, many brass-plate facilities have turned this subtle legal distinction to their own advantage. Banks established in certain offshore centers are technically considered "domestic" institutions. As a result, they escape federal reporting requirements.

Offshore banks established in the Northern Mariana Islands are perfect examples of how federal banking laws can be circumvented. First, understand that the Marianas enjoy the same legal status as U.S. state governments. This special standing allows them to capitalize on the United States' dual banking system—whereby state banking regulations supersede federal law. Put simply, offshore banks operating on these tiny islands are completely immune to many federal banking regulations, requirements, and restrictions.

If you own a bank in the Northern Marianas (or in any other foreign jurisdiction that enjoys a similar "state" status), your money matters are beyond the reach of domestic rules and regulations. Provided that your dealings are structured as "bank" transactions rather than as "individual" or "corporate" ones, the IRS has virtually no authority over the size or frequency of your money maneuvers.

You can also avoid reporting requirements by using offshore banks to transact your financial dealings in their name. Although the U.S. Treasury is informed of these dealings, it does not know the individuals involved—only the banks' names. The actual bank owners remain anonymous.

If financial privacy is in fact your paramount reason for owning an offshore bank, you can operate in ways that assure total anonymity. Simply decide to have the bank's ownership represented by bearer shares, which provide that the shareholders are the bank owners. And make certain that there are no registered shareholders on file anywhere. Your bank may also be operated by "nominee directors" who reside in your chosen offshore jurisdiction. Typically, these individuals are paid a nominal fee to act on behalf of the shareholders. By combining these two features, you achieve complete anonymity.

In the Name of Privacy

Privacy is often overlooked—even by shrewd investors. Don't allow yourself to make their mistake. Obviously, it would be naive to expect total privacy in all your money matters. But it would be foolish to allow unwarranted intrusion into financial matters that are no one's business but your own.

Be aware that there are degrees of financial privacy. Even in the United States, some transactions can be conducted in secrecy. Others involve lengthy disclosures and governmental red tape. If you resent the likelihood of your life becoming an open book, written to the tune of intrusive regulation, offshore banking may be just what the doctor ordered.

But whatever you do, be prudent in your offshore activities. Rash decisions based on insufficient information can lead to little more than investment headaches. There is a story that has made the rounds in investment circles, and concerns a man called Browning. In every way, he was impeccable. His appearance, home, office, car, and entire lifestyle exuded self-confidence and good taste. He reportedly flew every year to Italy—just to handpick the fabrics for his business suits. Every detail, in all things, was carefully considered.

It was the same in his financial dealings. He was a detail person. When he chose the jurisdiction for his offshore bank, he spent a lot of time and money making the right choice. He originally sought a tax haven because he so resented the IRS's invading his financial privacy. In order to avoid federal reporting requirements, he set up an eleborate system of corporations and trusts spread over several tax havens. But in his zeal to achieve total financial autonomy, Browning made a critical mistake. The company he hired to operate the bank was far from reputable. As a result, the tens of thousands he spent were lost and the company was never heard from again. Mr. Browning, the detail man, made a costly mistake. According to recent rumor, he still flies to Italy every year to handpick suit fabrics. But he relies on more reputable companies for his tax planning.

You don't have to be a Ted Browning. You can protect your privacy—legally. It just takes a lot of planning, a little time, and one offshore bank.

CHAPTER 6

TAX PROTECTION

Last year, a man named Gary Mead walked into my office. He had heard about my firm from a business associate, and hoped to solve a serious tax problem by organizing his own offshore bank. He told me about himself and his professional background. He explained that he had taken over his family's company when he was just twenty-eight, and had turned a small suburban print shop into a $2-million-a-year business. Throughout the '70s, he had diversified his assets by purchasing several pieces of investment property, starting a second and then a third venture, and opening a remarkably successful restaurant in Santa Barbara.

When I met him, he was in the middle of a real dilemma. Mead wanted to update and expand his printing business. He was confident the profit potential of modernizing his services would more than pay for itself. Clients were knocking on the door—more of them than his current staff and equipment could handle. He had already located a new building and had investigated press equipment here and abroad. He had the entire project mapped out and had raised the necessary capital with a master strategist's precision. But he knew that half of everything he made would wind up in Uncle Sam's pocket.

He had the ability to profit, but he did not want to proceed because so much of his labors would be eaten away in tax. His question to me was simple: "Can owning an offshore bank help?"

A similar incident underlines the deep anxiety and galling frustration that people feel over taxes. A retired couple approached me about personal taxes. Mr. and Mrs. Duval were realizing that their well-designed investment program was reaping great rewards—but most of them were going to the government via taxation. The Duvals were not seriously concerned about their own future, but they had always planned to leave the benefits of a large passive income to their three children. With the interest imposed on those assets, they worried about how much would actually be left to pass along to anyone. Their aim was to somehow protect investment income from heavy U.S. taxes, and they wondered if owning an offshore bank could offer that protection.

These cases only begin to illustrate the fear and misery people feel over excessive taxation. As Americans, we must accept not only that Uncle Sam wants a fair share of our present income, but that he may decide to ask for even more of it tomorrow. It is a truism that the United States was born out of a tax revolt. And it's irrelevant that the federal government never imposed income tax until 1913. Most of us are concerned about 1982. And today, some citizens pay as much as 70 percent of their annual earnings to the federal and state bureaucracy.

Oppressive taxation and the battle to overcome it are not new developments. Governments throughout history have always relied on monies from their citizenry to maintain an entire political apparatus. In virtually every case, people have opposed such taxation with all the weapons available to them. In times past, Hanseatic traders exercised their seagoing mobility to escape taxes. And when asked to pay an annual tax, medieval clergy and nobility alike threatened their kings with war.

We no longer have anything so romantic as seafaring tax rebels. We do, however, have offshore banks. Each and every year, hundreds of people from around the world investigate the notion of offshore banking because they are looking for a way to legally avoid paying taxes. They often find that by moving assets offshore, they can protect the money they would otherwise pay to the government. In light of these benefits, offshore banks situated in tax havens have assumed a pivotal role in the formulation of individual and corporate financial strategies.

It must be admitted from the start that the use of offshore banks has not always been used in legal and aboveboard ways. Some people have crossed subtle boundaries, and foolishly entered into a world of illegal tax evasion. But there is a difference between avoiding taxes and evading them. Tax avoidance implies the use of all legal means to cut down your tax burden. Tax evasion is the use of illegal means to achieve the same end. When, in order to reduce taxes, you ask your accountant to classify certain expenses as "business" expenditures, you are attempting legal tax avoidance. If, on the other hand, you intentionally fail to report part of your income because you want to reduce taxes, you have illegally evaded your responsibility.

Once you are fairly positive that you want to avoid paying certain taxes (particularly those imposed on your investment income), you will find that offshore tax havens offer amazing opportunity. I maintain that the tax savings they allow cannot be matched by any other contemporary approach.

Tax Laws

The importance of tax laws cannot be overstated. It is the arcane provisions of the U.S. Tax Code that cause you fiscal anguish and drive you to seek refuge in a haven. On the other hand, you are drawn to offshore centers because of their liberalized tax provisions. The interplay of these sets of laws is the key to your tax protection.

Unfortunately, the laws governing taxation in the United States are becoming more complex all the time. And you, the investor, must bear the brunt of this. It has reached the point where even specialists cannot fathom the intricacies of the code. According to many tax lawyers, the U.S. Tax Code is so incredibly complex that most of the top experts can no longer comprehend it. The City of New York Tax Committee Report released in the late 1960s found that the Code was beyond the understanding of the majority of tax specialists. (This was before new and more mysterious rules were added in the 1970s.)

The logical person would think that the best way to proceed for all concerned is to simplify the tax structure. In the long run this would seem to make the most sense. However, many observers think that the complexity is unavoidable. In an article which appeared in *The Tax Advisor* a few years ago, James Eustice had this to say about the tragic inevitability of tax complexity: "Our system has, for good or ill, chosen the

income tax as its primary instrument of fiscal policy. It is a
mass tax of extraordinarily broad coverage, applying to every
person and to almost every conceivable transaction. That is
going to create a complicated system because such an approach
must answer the following questions:

"What is going to be taxed? When will the tax be levied?
Who is going to be taxed? And how will the tax be levied—
namely, what is the rate of tax?"

The answers to these questions have a significant impact
on all investors. Usually the effects are on the negative side.
But don't expect any relief to come from the government itself.
Our tax system will not be simplified or made more equitable
in the near future. What can be done to alleviate the situation depends on the actions of individual investors.

Remember that the United States is only one of two nations in the world that tax your income wherever you are—
in this country or at the Arctic Circle, it makes no difference.
You are taxed for the privilege of being a citizen. Unless you
are willing to give up your U.S. citizenship, you will always
be constrained by U.S. tax law. For this reason, the laws and
tax codes must be understood as much as possible—given their
near incomprehensibility—before any action can be taken to
move assets out of the United States. As the noted financial
analyst, Robert Kinsman, puts it, domestic law and tax provisions are "the least personal, coldest, and most complicated
aspects of placing funds abroad. These are the most
critical . . . criteria in the whole issue of tax haven use."

By having a sense of the complexity and irreversible nature
of the U.S. tax system, an investor gains a greater appreciation of tax havens. It is much easier to see why these jurisdictions are designed to assist the investor and not impede him.
They are the escape valve for exorbitant taxes and repressed
capital. Some people may simply prefer them as a way to
maintain some distance between their assets and the ensnar-
ing conundrums of domestic tax law.

As you sift through various tax-cutting options, keep in mind that international tax planning is an extremely complex field. It requires a thorough knowledge of tax law—not just as it applies within the United States but as it functions in other countries as well. Even the simplest transaction will involve complete familiarity with the tax laws of at least three countries. This chapter cannot even begin to touch upon the specific intricacies of esoteric tax codes. There are entire volumes written just about the foreign-transaction provisions of the U.S. Tax Code. But these pages should prove that with careful forethought and good advice, you can legally reduce your current tax load.

Many people—particularly those with substantial assets to protect—regularly seek more than one opinion on the legality of a certain action. Regrettably, the established authorities inevitably disagree, and the concerned taxpayer is left to shuffle conflicting points of view. Of course, the labyrinthine composition of the tax structure is a hindrance. Yet, many problems arise because laws are written at the most general level. They involve sweeping generalizations, and do not apply to specific situations. As small comfort, know that the same legal ambiguity you curse with one breath allows the tax loophole you relish with the next.

If you face tax problems, you should not hesitate to utilize so-called loopholes. Most of them were brought into existence by laws originally designed to carry out some legislative aim. If a law intended to increase exports or permit domestic business to compete favorably with foreign competition also allows for creative tax avoidance, capitalize on its benefits. There is absolutely nothing wrong with utilizing a loophole— until it is actually closed.

Every tax-savings effort necessitates aggressive planning and the willingness to take advantage of unintended legal or administrative loopholes. International experts agree—at least in this instance—that within the parameters of U.S. tax law, there is ample opportunity to reduce and sometimes eliminate certain taxation. So long as concerned investors stay firmly footed on legal ground, they are fully entitled to whatever tax savings they enjoy. I think that the time has come for people to act decisively. You should discover tax loopholes and utilize their strategic advantage.

Due to the tax laws and the uniqueness of each situation, it is virtually impossible to outline a specific tax-avoidance plan that would be effective in every situation. Furthermore, if one such plan did exist, it is entirely possible that the IRS would learn of it and rule against it. Therefore, planning of this type must be done in accordance with the variation of business that each bank conducts.

It is you, the investor, who must determine the relative importance of tax protection. How badly do you want to avoid taxes? Once you have decided to take this course, it will entail the tailoring of your whole investment strategy. It is an important benefit. For some people, it is the only worthwhile benefit of offshore banking. But regardless of where it stands on your list of investment priorities, taxes will have a lasting effect on your financial future.

Using Tax Havens

When most people think of a tax haven, serene images usually come to mind. A safe harbor nestled in the tropical beauty of some small Caribbean island. White sand and dark rum on the rocks.

If that is your fantasy, you are in good company. Just about every language has created a word for these offshore sanctuaries. In French they are known as *un paradise fiscal*—a tax paradise. The Germans call them *eine steuroase*—a tax oasis. All these terms are appropriate, and coined by investors and tax travelers seeking shelter from the rough seas of taxation.

The experts are not in full agreement about the exact nature of a tax haven. In the simplest terms, a tax haven is any country that imposes a lower tax rate than you find at home. You may find your dream spot in Bermuda, where the government imposes little or no income tax. Or in Hong Kong, where special tax breaks apply to income from foreign sources. In practice, tax havens also include countries that impose generally high or normal taxes on resident income but grant special tax benefits on capital gains or investment income.

In this sense, nearly every country could qualify as a tax haven for some purpose. For instance, many countries have industrial-incentive and export-encouragement laws that grant long-term deferrals, reductions, or outright exemptions to corporations organizing new manufacturing plants within the nation. Would you believe that even the United States is considered a tax haven? It is—for foreign depositors who earn interest from U.S. financial institutions. The single characteristic that makes any country an attractive tax haven is that it imposes little or no taxes on the specific transaction you have in mind.

Tax havens are also tolerated to a certain degree by the large industrialized nations. Multinational corporations must attract funds from foreign money markets. Since countries like the United States impose a withholding tax on interest payments made to foreign lenders, these corporations must find another route to obtain their money. Thus, we get the use of tax havens with tax-free provisions on such transactions. The industrialized country accepts this form of borrowing so as to retain its withholding rate and, at the same time, see to it that its native companies remain financially healthy. It's a trade-off. And because of this financial *quid pro quo*, tax havens have become a major element in capital market considerations.

For the individual investor, tax havens serve a special need as well. To understand the crucial need for tax planning, you must understand a very important distinction regarding different forms of income. Basically, you can earn money in one of two ways: either as return on labor or as return on capital. Return on labor comes from salary, wages, fees for professional services, and other kindred sources. Tax havens can be of moderate use in avoiding tax on such income.

But the second return—return on capital—applies to money earned on investments: interest on savings deposits, loans, and bonds; rental income; patents; dividends on stocks; or royalties. If your financial portfolio includes such holdings, a tax haven may be the start of something big!

Unless an investor makes some arrangements to protect investment income, the government will tax it in the same way it taxes salary and other wages. When investments are small, the tax load will be proportionately manageable. But at a certain level of investment your tax bracket begins to soar, and you are likely to find yourself eager for some way to protect your assets.

Tax havens are designed for an income. They help protect your money from federal and state taxes because they effectively separate it from you. This simple fact strikes at the heart of all tax-avoidance strategy: in order to protect assets, you must "alienate" yourself from them. This means that you must transfer them to a different legal entity that, by location, is subject to lower taxes. Offshore banks are exemplary tax-haven vehicles because they separate you from your holdings. And at the same time they allow you absolute control over the movement and activity of your money.

Remember, an offshore bank is as much a legal entity as you are. Therefore, in the eyes of the IRS and other government agencies, if you own an offshore bank, its assets, liabilities, and income are its own. In practical terms, if your investments are owned by a foreign holding company, then the company—not you, the individual investor—owns them. Any tax due on that company's holdings falls to the company itself.

This may at first seem like an insignificant distinction, but never underestimate its importance. Grasping all that it entails marks the beginning of your investment freedom. The essence of using a tax haven for tax-avoidance or tax-reduction purposes is the creation of legal entities with the following characteristics:

- They are separate from their creator by guaranteeing that the income they receive from their investments cannot be considered part of his income.

- They "reside" in countries where the tax situation is much better than in their creator's home country.

- They can be controlled by their creator, and their assets managed by him as he sees fit, without tax liability in his home country.

Such businesses exemplify the basic idea of separating ownership and control: alienation. Once your portfolio has been vested in an offshore bank or company, you no longer have title to it. But since you have title to the stock in the bank or company, you have the power to make decisions about the ways its assets are used.

Many people wonder what happens to investments and assets that are transferred offshore to the new bank or other financial entity. I am often asked: how do I get my capital and other assets back?

If an asset is transferred offshore, it may be freely brought back or repatriated without a tax consequence—provided it has not increased its value. Profit or gains accumulating offshore in a bank are not taxed. By and large, however, investors want to keep assets out of the country. In the process, they gain use of the bank's profits (without tax consequences) in one of two ways: either they begin making loans in accordance with U.S. tax regulations, or they begin making additional portfolio investments.

There are two types of tax havens and you should be familiar with both. "Pure" havens—sometimes referred to as no-tax havens—impose no tax whatsoever on any kind of income. The governments of no-tax-haven countries earn their revenue from corporations doing business in the locale. The stamp duties on articles of incorporation, perhaps a small charge on the value of the corporate shares, or annual registration fees constitute their profits. The no-tax havens worth noting are Andorra, the Bahamas, Bermuda, Cayman Islands, Campione, Nauru, Vanuatu, and the Turks and Caicos Islands. Each of these jurisdictions has what is known as a "no-tax treaty," which means that they do not have any double-taxation agreements with other countries.

"Low-tax" havens also exist. They combine favorable tax treaties and relatively low tax rates. Some of the best low-tax havens include the British Virgin Islands, Channel Islands, Isle of Man, Liechtenstein, and Montserrat. If considerations other than tax avoidance motivate your offshore venture, you may be willing to sacrifice some tax relief for other features available in these jurisdictions.

There is a third category of offshore-banking locations. Countries such as Panama and Costa Rica are not thought of as tax havens in the strictest sense. They do not, however, tax foreign-source income. For instance, a Panamanian corporation will be taxed on its income generated within the country. But if it generates income elsewhere—let's say in the United States—it won't be subject to Panamanian taxes. In other words, special concessions are made to certain kinds of companies under certain conditions.

The best way to use a tax haven depends entirely upon your particular circumstances, objectives, and concerns. Each location has its own set of advantages and uses. Some jurisdictions are very attractive to single individuals, but utterly unappealing to corporations and trust companies. Monaco, for example, is a favored tax haven for individuals because there is no income tax. But it certainly wouldn't appeal to a company in search of an offshore subsidiary site. Such a firm would be subject to a 35-percent tax on its profits if more than a quarter of its turnover were realized outside the principality. On the other hand, Jersey, an island off the coast of England, is one of the best havens for nonresident companies. With a little imagination and a lot of planning, a knowledgeable tax traveler could combine the tax features of both Monaco and Jersey and enjoy the best of all possible worlds.

Before deciding on your own tax haven or offshore financial center, you must determine precisely what you want to accomplish. These early decisions will save you time, trouble, and money later in the game. If you decide that your greatest incentive for moving offshore is tax protection, you can begin investigating various jurisdictional options. Your individual tax needs will be met best by certain centers and not as well by others. So take the time and learn all you can about several different tax bases. Compare the key elements in each, and seek experienced consultants to help you make a final choice. Above all, always update your information. Change is constant in the offshore financial world.

A Short Primer on Tax Treaties

To avoid double taxation and to prevent tax evasion, the United States has negotiated international treaties with a number of foreign governments. These agreements specify that tax information is to be freely exchanged between signatories, but recent history has shown that the data obtained are of little help in pursuing criminal cases. As a result, the treaties add only the slightest punch to domestic tax authority.

Over the years, enterprising investors from around the world have managed to turn these international agreements to their own advantage. Individuals and companies based in treaty-bound countries have intelligently capitalized on the fact that such compacts modify their own domestic tax law and, in effect, reduce a tax that would otherwise be imposed on their foreign investments. What's more, they have learned to use the treaties binding other countries and, in the process, reduce the tax on loans extended to international borrowers. For instance, if a West German lender wishes to loan money to a U.S. borrower, he may decide to funnel it through a Netherlands Antilles company. In this way, he can take full advantage of the treaty provisions that hold for transactions between the United States and the Antilles.

Multinational companies in particular have learned to combine the U.S.-treaty network with tax havens. And their efforts have reaped lucrative rewards. By borrowing money through Antilles finance subsidiaries, these corporations have escaped a heavy tax on their interest payments.

In 1978, $4.5 billion in gross income left the United States in interest payments to non-U.S. residents. Of that total amount, $3.9 billion (or 89 percent) was paid to treaty countries. And, as a further indication of just how well this tax reduction method can work, half of that sum (or $1.8 billion) went to treaty countries that are also tax havens. And that was four years ago!

It is worth noting that because these statistics are available to the general public, the Treasury Department, IRS, and Congress, tax treaties with tax havens are continuously under attack. In the government's opinion, $1.8 billion is just the tip of the iceberg.

In order to be sure your offshore tax plan is safe, I recommend avoiding the use of high-profile tax-treaty/tax haven countries such as the Netherland Antilles. Instead, use little known treaty havens, such as Montserrat, Barbados, and New Zealand (the Cook Islands).

Even better, little-known tax havens such as the Mariana Islands and Guam have a special provision in the Internal Revenue Code (Section 1442(c)) that permits offshore payments of interest, dividends and royalties to avoid withholding tax.

As mentioned, the most well-known example of a tax haven/treaty country is the Netherlands Antilles. These islands are considered quite unique in the circles of international finance. Most major European banks maintain offices there and offshore-investment activity never ceases. The tax regulations are almost as complex as in the United States, but they hold a real advantage to U.S. citizens via the tax treaty.

As you know by now, interest payments made by U.S. borrowers to their foreign lenders are subject to a 30-percent withholding tax. Needless to say, most foreign lenders refuse to share that much of each interest payment with Uncle Sam. To work around this problem, U.S. borrowers have proposed more attractive tax arrangements.

A smart U.S. corporation seeking foreign capital can establish a bank in the Mariana Islands that will borrow money from overseas. In turn, the bank can lend that same money to the parent company. With regard to tax, the important issue is "reverse flow"—that is, how the interest is treated when it is paid back. The interest paid by the parent to the subsidiary is deductible for U.S. tax purposes and exempt from U.S. withholding tax.

The preceding example is just one of several structures used to avoid U.S. taxes through the use of offshore banks.

How Interest Expense Is Created

The basic point is that any effective tax-avoidance strategy is carefully and cautiously formulated. Haphazard attempts to escape IRS enforcement often lead to embarrassing and costly audits. So, be thorough. Consider options. And assume responsibility for the tax structure that is best for you.

IRS Tax Traps and Offshore Exemptions

The tax benefits of tax havens are extended only to the entity within their taxing jurisdiction. For example, a Cayman Islands corporation may be excused from tax in the Caymans, but it may not be excused from tax if it operates in the United States under its taxing jurisdiction. Generally, tax havens only reduce or eliminate tax at the corporate level.

In addition, since tax-haven benefits only operate on a corporate level, the IRS has the taxing jurisdiction to impose any restriction or tax on any U.S. shareholder that has an interest in such an entity. The IRS defines a U.S. shareholder as any person owning more than 5 percent of a tax-haven corporation.

The Barriers

To get the most satisfaction from your offshore bank's strategic advantage, you should take a few moments to understand the various obstacles that individuals face when they attempt tax avoidance. By knowing what they confront, you are reminded of just how much your offshore bank is really able to offer you.

- Section 1491 of the Internal Revenue Code excise tax is a U.S.-imposed tax equal to 37.5 percent of the value of property transferred by gift to a foreign trust as a capital contribution to a foreign corporation. In other words, it is a 37.5-percent difference between the fair market value and your tax basis. The tax was first imposed many years ago, but experts contend that, given recent changes in our domestic tax code, it is no longer relevant.

- Taxation of foreign trusts as grantor trusts is another barrier to tax avoidance. As you may know, an American citizen could, at one time, form a foreign trust in Bermuda (an irrevocable trust), transfer assets to it, and—relevant to U.S. tax purposes—the trust would gain equal legal status with the citizens of Cayman. But in 1976, that law was changed to provide that any American transferring assets to a foreign trust would be subject to tax on the income earned by that foreign trust attributable to the money or assets that had been transferred to the trust.

- The Foreign Personal Holding Company (FPHC) tax was adopted quite some time ago. It was meant to attack incorporated pocketbooks in tax havens receiving passive income. It applies in cases where the stock of a foreign corporation is owned by no more than five U.S. individuals, and applies only in the case of passive income. When these conditions exist, all shareholders (technically, everyone who receives a benefit from money in the company) are taxed as if the offshore corporation did not exist. This barrier is an ironclad one. There is simply no legal way around it without a bank.

- The Personal Holding Company (PHC) tax—imposed at the rate of 70 percent—applies to domestic as well as foreign corporations. It is incurred directly by the company and not by any of the company's shareholders. In the case of a tax-haven corporation, it applies to closely held haven corporations. And is imposed on all relevant (U.S. source) passive income.

- The Controlled Foreign Corporation (CFC) tax is yet another barrier to tax avoidance. This applies to foreign corporations owned either by U.S. corporations or individuals. It takes a hefty share of various passive incomes from each shareholder, all of whom are treated as if the corporation did not exist.

- The Accumulated Earnings (AE) tax applies to both foreign and U.S. corporations. It taxes all accumulated earnings considered unnecessary for the business of the corporation. It imposes a penalty tax on those earnings that cannot be justifiably retained.

- A Foreign Investment Company (FIC) tax is annually imposed on every foreign corporation whose main purpose is to invest in stocks or commodity futures. I am aware of only one penalty charge pursuant to this particular tax: when you sell company shares, you are taxed at the ordinary income rates rather than at the capital-gains rate.

- Section 482 of the Internal Revenue Code is the transfer pricing rule. If you sell goods to (or buy them from) a tax-haven entity, and the prices are not in keeping with economic reality, then the IRS can use this section to reallocate profits away from the tax haven and back to you.

- U.S. tax on U.S.-source income is imposed on a foreign corporation if it receives income from interest, dividends, rents, and royalties, and other forms of passive income. If these sources of income are effectively connected with a trade or business within the U.S., then the foreign corporation is taxed in the U.S. like a domestic corporation. If the corporation is not connected with a trade or business, then the U.S. imposes a withholding tax on the payor at a rate of 30 percent, unless reduced by a tax treaty or the requirement to withhold is exempted by statute.

- Finally, let's look at Section 269 of the Internal Revenue Code. This particular provision in the tax code has not been used by the IRS, but the Gordon Report recommended that it be made a regular audit consideration. Basically, the section says that if you form a corporation for the prime purpose of avoiding taxes, the IRS may be able to disregard the existence of that particular corporation. We'll have to wait and see what action, if any, is taken on this recommendation. The Gordon Report inspired various international tax provisions in the big tax-increase bill signed into law by President Reagan in September, 1982. But there was no measure to expand or enforce Section 269.

The Exemptions for Offshore Banks

In view of such traps, the special tax exemptions extended to banks operating within tax-haven locales seem all the more valuable. By operating through your own offshore bank, you effectively avoid the difficulties faced by individual investors and corporations.

The reason that special exemptions exist for offshore banks is no mystery. Back in 1962, when President Kennedy urged Congress to prevent Americans from using tax havens, legislation was introduced that essentially taxed American individuals and corporations who owned a controlling interest in any foreign corporation. The banking industry got wind of this and told Congress that if their foreign subsidiaries were taxed at a shareholder level, they would not be able to compete with their foreign counterparts. Congress was convinced and essentially installed a series of tax breaks for banks owned by Americans and operating outside the U.S.

These privileges apply to a merchant bank that purchases and sells stock as an underwriter; acts as an investment advisor, merger consultant, business manager; or engages in a broad range of manufacturing and business activities outside the U.S. Here is a capsule of each special privilege.

Avoiding CFC Tax

Normally, when no more than ten U.S. shareholders own a foreign corporation, they are all subject to current U.S. tax on their proportionate share of that corporation's worldwide interests, dividends, and royalties. But, the U..S. shareholders of an offshore bank will, in most cases, be able to utilize the exemption from Controlled Foreign Corporation (CFC) tax because their corporation conducts banking business.

Under the Foreign Personal Holding Company (FPHC) provisions of the Internal Revenue Code, foreign banks may receive from the IRS a special exemption from FPHC taxes. The exemption will be granted if the bank can show that it was created for some express purpose other than avoiding the tax.

Avoiding AE Tax

Ordinarily, a foreign-based corporation is subject to U.S.

tax rates—which can range up to 38 percent on undistributed U.S.-source accumulated earnings in excess of $150,000 per year. But an offshore bank can usually qualify for exemption from this tax because all banks—in the everyday course of business—must accumulate earnings in order to make portfolio investments.

Avoiding PHC Tax

A foreign corporation (owned by less than ten U.S. shareholders) is ordinarily subject to a U.S. personal-holding-company tax at a rate of 70 percent on undistributed U.S.-source dividends, interest, and royalties. Offshore banks avoid this tax because their incomes are not regarded as passive.

Avoiding FIC Tax

All U.S. shareholders of a foreign corporation (which is primarily engaged in stock investment or commodity futures) are, upon sale of their shares, subject to a foreign investment company taxes. In such cases, the tax is imposed at ordinary income rates of up to 70 percent, rather than at capital-gains rates. But, in most cases, the shareholders of an offshore bank will be exempt from these provisions.

Avoiding "Effectively-Connected-with-U.S." Tax

An ordinary foreign corporation will be subject to U.S. tax on U.S.-source income if that income is "effectively connected with a U.S. business." An offshore bank is usually exempt from this tax because its activities are, to a large extent, treated for tax purposes as if they were conducted offshore through a resident agent. Offshore banks established in tax treaty jurisdictions can avoid the withholding tax on U.S.-source income. Banks established in Guam or the Mariana Islands can avoid withholding tax because of a special exemption in the IRC.

In short, offshore banks enjoy very special tax exemptions—especially with regard to investment. Their special status allows them and their owners to legally avoid taxes while earning a handsome profit. If you want to use off-shore tax havens for tax protection, in my opinion, an off-shore bank is the way to go.

Now that I have presented the special exemptions in the Internal Revenue Code for offshore banks, the next question is, how can you, the investor or businessman, take advantage of them. The first application of these exemptions takes place when you plan the ownership of an offshore entity. As discussed, if a U.S. shareholder were to own 10 percent or more of a foreign corporation, the corporation would be classified as both a CFC and FPHC.

However, if one person were to own an offshore bank, he could avoid both the CFC and FPHC tax penalties by con-ducting a banking business and making certain that no more than 40 percent of the income of the bank was FPHC income.

Using an Offshore Bank to Create Interest Expense

Once the ownership and income requirements have been met so that the offshore bank is not subject to CFC or FPHC tax, you can use this creative technique with the offshore bank. The bank then lends that money back to you at the highest possible market rates. You pay interest to the bank, which is currently deductible. Then, with the money loaned to you by the bank, you deposit it again with the bank and the bank again lends the money back to you. You then pay the bank interest on the second loan, which is deductible. The interest payments received by the bank are tax-free. They accumulate offshore, and can be reinvested over and over again tax-free.

How Much Can You Save?

The biggest expense you will pay as a corporation or in-dividual is taxes. The more money you make, the more taxes you pay, because additional taxable income places you in a higher tax bracket. Therefore, your goal should be to first reduce your taxable income as much as possible, and second, to invest your after-tax money carefully, so as to avoid being placed into a higher tax bracket. The following example demonstrates how your earnings are eroded by tax on after-tax income.

Let's assume you are a professional employed at a company. If your salary is $100,000 per year, the IRS takes 50 percent of that in tax immediately. The remaining $50,000 you invest in a money-market fund paying 10 percent per annum. Therefore, you make $5,000 in income from your investment, and now have to pay the IRS an additional $2,500, or half, in tax because you are in the 50-percent bracket.

Solutions to Tax Problems

The Internal Revenue Code is complicated. Its complexity provides the opportunity to plan offshore transactions in a number of ways. Some methods are safer than others. The techniques discussed in this book have a legal basis and are within the law. The exemptions in the Internal Revenue Code for offshore banks can be the basis for your tax-avoidance plan.

At the beginning of this chapter, Gary Mead was seeking answers to some rather serious tax problems. Like many other businessmen, he didn't want to proceed with his project unless he could legally avoid being taxed.

Gary found that he could not use an offshore structure to avoid the taxes on his business directly, but could use an offshore bank to control his taxes.

By using an offshore bank he was able to charge his domestic company with interest expense that was deductible—and thus lowered taxes. The interest income earned by the offshore bank was earned tax-free. Even better, the income accumulated by his bank was able to be invested in other projects free of tax, now that his money was effectively offshore.

I suspect that initially Gary was a bit reticent to move money offshore. Although he never said as much, I sensed that the process was somewhat overwhelming to him. He did not fancy himself an international banker, and was about as diversified as he wanted to be. The thought of tackling his own bank was a major step, but he had little choice. Like so many offshore bank owners, he needed offshore banking to solve an immediate problem.

I talked with him at a seminar we held recently. He said that things in the printing business are just fine and getting even better. He is thinking about expanding his scope of professional concern one step further, and may soon publish a weekly entertainment guide to Los Angeles and San Francisco.

As for the Duvals, they, too, decided to set up an offshore bank. Besides using their bank as the legal owner of all the family investments, they have set up a trust for their three children and five grandchildren, and are seriously considering the idea of building a small home on the islands. "After all," Mr. Duval told me, "it would be a lovely place for our sunset years."

CHAPTER 7

RATING OFFSHORE
BANKING CENTERS

About three years ago, a client called me—for the fifth time in two days. Dave Brooks had been thinking about the possibility of establishing his own brass-plate bank for quite some time. He had attended two of our seminars and had met with me personally on a number of occasions. But he seemed unable to make the final commitment. Frankly, I was beginning to feel that Dave liked the concept of offshore banking more than the reality. His phone call changed my mind.

"All right," he said, "I'm sold. When do we start?"

After teasing him mercilessly about the lengthy decision-making process, I asked about the jurisdiction he found most appealing.

"I haven't really thought about it," he shot back. "But I will."

That was not the response I had wanted to hear. Knowing Dave's approach to things, I was afraid he might spend several more months pondering the pros and cons of each offshore center. And, in the end, still remain undecided. So, I quickly arranged to have dinner with him, suggesting that we review the good, the bad, and the ugly of various offshore options.

It turned out to be an excellent meeting.

When you feel you have a fairly firm hold on offshore banking—what it is, how it works, and why you stand to benefit from its financial features—you should begin a serious comparison of various foreign centers. Remember, no single jurisdiction can offer you everything. But some offshore sites offer more client convenience than others. The point is, different locations offer different benefits. Not every man wears a size 40 medium. And not every investment portfolio needs the same financial aid. Without a calculated balance between your strategic needs and various offshore locations, your decision to move assets out of the country will be little more than a stab in the dark.

Ideally, you should maintain your funds close to home. For one thing, by banking nearby, you tend to share the same time zone with your offshore banker or resident agent. Nothing can quite strain a working relationship like waking your foreign representative at 4:00 A.M. (his time) with instructions to transfer $40,000 into your New York account. What's more, knowing that your money is within a few hours' air time affords you a sense of psychological comfort. And who knows when some economic emergency would make it imperative that your liquid assets be close at hand.

For these reasons, most North and South American investors opt for one of the Caribbean islands. Europeans, on the other hand, tend to work through centers on their own continent. There are exceptions. For instance, if a Latin American businessman were heavily involved in the Australian or Japanese stock market, he would probably want his financial base somewhere in the Pacific. Relatively few U.S. investors now own banks in Asia. But as international business activity becomes increasingly centered on the Far East, we will likely see more offshore facilities established in that part of the world.

Aside from proximity, there is maneuverability to consider. With your money marooned on some slow-circuit desert island, you lose one of offshore banking's greatest benefits: profit potential. Always look for a location that allows you to move your funds swiftly and efficiently, because as lucrative opportunities break in various parts of the world, you will want to transfer assets. Money based in London, for example, can be moved virtually anywhere. And once investment profit has been earned, it can be easily returned to its "home base." Unfortunately, this ready transfer service is not available from every offshore center. So, be careful.

When reviewing different offshore havens, consider issues of political stability and analyze relative currency strengths. In some countries, political change occurs gradually. In others, a military coup can build as quickly as a tropical hurricane. In regularly comparing jurisdictions, I am always left with the same conclusion: no offshore center offers complete political stability. Whether you decide to bank in the Bahamas,

Mexico, Canada, or even the United States, change is inevitable. As a result, the intelligent investor walks into every financial involvement with his eyes open. He moves assets offshore, transfers them into various investment programs, earns money. And moves on.

To maximize offshore opportunity, you will need foresight, creativity, flexibility, and capital. Foresight—because rash decisions reap meager rewards. Think ahead . . . before you find yourself trapped by circumstances that work against your financial interests. Creativity—because offshore banking is an art form all its own. You can play the scene as it's been played before. But the investor who makes it his own becomes a star. Flexibility—because wise investments call for calculated elasticity. To gamble successfully in the world of offshore finance, you must be able to bend, tapping into opportunities whenever (and wherever) they occur. And capital—because just about everything is easier when you have a cozy cushion to fall back on. With your assets diversified and profitably invested, you can't help but convey the sense of confident calm that predicates all wise money decisions.

The Most Important Factors

If you are exclusively interested in an offshore bank account—that is, in being a customer with an established facility—you should find the selection process relatively easy. By following the instructions detailed in Chapter 2 (under "A Preferred Customer"), you will obtain plenty of brochures, financial statements, and enough bank history to narrow your choices down to just two or three different jurisdictional options.

My strongest suggestion would be this: when you are prepared to make a final decision, make certain that you feel at ease with your new bank's international reputation. If you enter into an offshore involvement with serious reservations, the relationship won't last long. Even more important, you will be left with a nasty memory of anxiety and confusion.

At the same time, don't make more of the decision than it deserves. Excessive deliberation does not necessarily lead to the best choice. Investigate several banks initially; narrow your choices; gather additional information from friends, associates, and an experienced consultant. And then make a choice.

Although individual priorities cannot be predetermined, Bermuda has proven a desirable, well-established jurisdiction offering rigid stability, stringent banking laws, and an unblemished reputation in the international banking community.

For the more experienced investor (who looks at offshore banking as the means to substantial profit, privacy, and tax protection) there are deeper issues involved. If you are such an individual, then buying or establishing your own private facility may be in order. You will want to explore far more complex factors before deciding on the most appropriate banking site. In general, be aware of eight main considerations as you sort through various jurisdictional options:

(1) How easily can you enter the jurisdiction?

(2) Does the center have its own tax law? And how well does that law match your needs?

(3) Will you need to pay cash up-front before starting a bank in the jurisdiction?

(4) Is this location a desirable vacation spot?

(5) What sort of reputation does the center have vis-a-vis U.S. banks?

(6) Can the location offer efficient banking facilities?

(7) What sort of financial privacy can the center ensure?

(8) Does the jurisdiction have monetary ties with the United States?

Too often, investors recognize the relevant concerns, but aren't able to gather enough of the right information for themselves. Again, don't underestimate the services of a professional offshore consultant. There is no reason that you should be aware of all the subtleties that impact on a good or bad location choice—and there is no reason that your consultant should not be.

With a consultant (or without one) think about ease of entry. Be forewarned that endless red tape remains the Achilles' heel of many offshore endeavors. Do not make the mistake of applying for a bank license in any jurisdiction that bogs you down with needless entry requirements. If a foreign center is worthy of your financial involvement, it will go out of its way to ensure easy access and a fast route to profit.

Next, concern yourself with tax law. Does the center under consideration impose tax on profits, capital gains, or other forms of bank income? As noted in the preceding chapter, every appealing offshore center functions as a tax paradise. Choose only from among centers that levy no taxes.

And what about a paid-in capital requirement? Some foreign governments demand that you contribute cash to your bank in the form of consideration for shares, even before you receive an operating license. Unless you are without options, avoid any such situations. Remember: you must have a license before you can begin taking deposits or extending loans. Most investors are not willing to invest a sizable amount of cash up-front because they prefer to utilize liquid assets in a more profitable way. For them, financial centers such as Montserrat and Vanuatu are the most appealing.

You can't imagine how many investors care about—but may be hesitant to admit that they even consider—the vacation appeal of their potential offshore jurisdiction. When you plan to commit time and energy to any project, you should be concerned about how well you like the environment in which you will be working. You should never establish a bank on any island or in any foreign principality that you find unwelcome. After all, you will be visiting your bank every now and then. And how appropriate that you should use the opportunity to combine business with pleasure!

There is another cosmetic consideration involved. What about prospective depositors who want to develop a firsthand impression of the jurisdiction? Your success as well as your comfort will multiply in relation to the physical attractiveness of your offshore center. Luckily, most Caribbean islands, and some centers in the Pacific, are absolutely beautiful vacation spots.

I cannot stress it often enough: when you select an offshore locale, think about international reputation. Over the years, a few jurisdictions have been robbed of their good names by fraudulent users issuing phony financial documents, bogus cashier's checks, and illegal letters of credit. The vast majority of foreign centers are extremely reputable. But don't take any chances. Be sure to pick a jurisdiction that enjoys a good reputation—particularly among U.S. banks. The initial effort will more than pay off in subsequent bank-to-bank transactions.

For the most part, sophisticated investors know how to shop for offshore banking efficiency. But, occasionally, someone makes a fatal error. In today's world of instantaneous telex and shrinking professional distance, no jurisdiction—regardless of location—is considered "in the boondocks" if it offers adequate facilities. Ready access to top-notch lawyers, expert accounting services, and excellent communication systems will ensure the best local attention to your banking priorities. By contrast, inefficient facilities mar your transactions, cause unnecessary and costly delays, and wreak havoc on your operation. You certainly don't want to disable your bank before it has a chance to return your investment.

As you already know, financial privacy is at the heart of offshore banking. But in practice, some jurisdictions are more secrecy-oriented than others. If you seek to bank incognito, you should consciously select a foreign center that nurtures comprehensive bank secrecy law.

The last main factor to consider when selecting your off-shore center concerns the future as well as the present. Does your preferred jurisdiction maintain economic ties to the United States? If it does, then listen well: as President Reagan's recent Caribbean Aid Plan demonstrates, monetary ties to the U.S. carry with them some very powerful strings. For instance, under the stipulations of the Reagan proposal, the IRS may soon be able to "break" the wall of secrecy that traditionally has surrounded several international tax havens. More about this later in the chapter. But for now, suffice it to say you should pick a foreign center with no monetary ties to the United States.

It may be that when you analyze your financial portfolio, and determine the features you want in an offshore bank site, you will come face to face with pragmatic limitations. If you find that no single center can provide all your needs, you still have options. You can prioritize the benefits you seek and sacrifice less essential luxuries for the paramount necessities. Or, if you have a more developed sense of adventure, you can establish two (or even three) offshore facilities. And blend the best of each into a financial tapestry, woven from the threads of intelligent investment strategy.

The Best Offshore Centers

There are forty-five separate foreign jurisdictions that, in one way or another, can be classified as tax havens or off-shore banking centers. The vast majority of them are concentrated in either the Caribbean or the Pacific islands. In my opinion, the twelve best are Anguilla, Netherlands Antilles, the Mariana Islands, British Virgin Islands, Cayman Islands, Hong Kong, Bahamas, Barbados, Montserrat, Panama, Vanuatu, and Turks and Caicos.

Based on the factors reviewed above, let's compare them. I think the overview will prove helpful, should you ultimately decide to operate your own offshore facility.

One Country to Avoid: Anguilla

Anguilla is a 36-square-mile coral island located approximately 1,200 miles southeast of Miami. Unfortunately, there is just one air connection between the island and the continental United States. It is a British colony and has a resident population of 6,000. The local currency is the Eastern Caribbean dollar, divided into 100 cents. Although it enjoys remarkably low humidity—at least by Caribbean standards—and can boast of beautiful, clean beaches, Anguilla is considered one of the Caribbean's least desirable vacation spots.

Local government is anxious to transform the area into a major international tax haven. As a result, offshore banking is wholeheartedly encouraged. One major problem is its reputation. Scores of promoters are setting up paper offshore banks and are using them for fraudulent purposes.

In my opinion, Anguilla's entry requirements are too relaxed. And individuals unable to win acceptance in other places have utilized the area as a base of operation. Because of the island's lax attitude regarding the issuance of offshore bank licenses, its reputation among U.S. bankers is rather blemished. According to participating investors, poor communications systems predominate.

In short, and despite Anguilla's geographic advantage, an overall comparison would rank it near the bottom of a prudent investor's list.

Bahamas

The Bahamas comprise an independent nation within the British Commonwealth, and are home to some 200,000 full-time residents. A 700-mile-long archipelago in the Caribbean, the islands are perhaps the oldest and most well-established offshore banking center in the region and remain one of the world's favorite vacation spots.

This financial center imposes no taxes—on profits, corporate income, or capital gains. It enforces stringent secrecy laws, and maintains a favorable attitude toward offshore banking. The Bahamas enjoy an excellent relationship with U.S. banks. The jurisdiction is second only to London as a base for Eurodollar transactions, thus local communications systems (i.e., telephone, telex, and mail) are first-class.

The Bahamas should probably rank at the top of your option list if you are interested only in becoming an offshore bank customer. But because local government is reticent to issue a bank license to individuals or small corporations, the islands would be a poor choice for the single investor or small consortium. Know, too, that $1 million is required as paid-in capital, and the annual license fee is $6,000.

Barbados

This island is also situated in the eastern Caribbean, near Trinidad and Tabagos. It is considered an exquisite vacation spot—even by the highest standards. And there are a number of direct flights available from the United States.

The quality of local banking regulation is generally considered to be poor. As standard policy, the government issues bank licenses only to established financial institutions, and the annual renewel fee is $13,000. Moreover, the island's $1 million paid-in-capital requirement dissuades most individual investors.

A Barbados bank is subject to a small tax on its income. However, a tax treaty with the United States stipulates that all interest payments (remitted to the island) shall forego withholding taxes.

The area's communications systems are considered good, and its infrastructure is fair. Nonetheless, Barbados would not be the best choice for individually owned-and-operated banks. Given government disinterest and the heavy capital investment required, I would suggest you look elsewhere.

British Virgin Islands

The British Virgin Islands (B.V.I.) are located some 60 miles east of Puerto Rico. They actually include more than 60 different islands, but their total land area amounts to just 69 square miles of largely uninhabited rock and sand. Their neighbor islands—St. Thomas, St. John, and St. Croix—come under the political authority of the United States. But due to proximity and shared tradition, the two island groups have established strong economic and social bonds.

Although the B.V.I. government claims to favor offshore financial development, it imposes stringent entry requirements on individual bank owners. I suspect that the ambivalence stems from island fears about potentially fraudulent users. At any rate, an annual license fee costs $4,500 and the paid-in-capital requirement is $125,000.

Local tax laws are appealing: there is no tax at all imposed on profits, income, or capital gains. And, because of a tax treaty between the United States and the B.V.I., no withholding tax is imposed on interest payments remitted to a local bank.

In sum, this British colony rates somewhat better than the other sites we've reviewed. But not well enough.

Cayman Islands

Like Anguilla and the British Virgin Islands, the Caymans—Grand Cayman, Cayman Brac, and Little Cayman—are a British colony. They are located less than 500 miles south of Miami, and air connections from the United States are direct. Cayman Brac, in particular, offers vacationers a spectacular beach-resort environment.

The Caymans are a politically stable country. Communications systems are well above average, and accessibility to other financial centers is excellent. An offshore bank established here will enjoy the very best in telephone, telex, and mail-delivery services.

The islands' banking infrastructure is considered excellent; ample facilities are available, and legal regulations are well respected throughout the world. Unfortunately, the Cayman government makes it nearly impossible for an eager investor to start a new bank anywhere within the jurisdiction. Charters and licenses are available only to established banks, and to the tune of $500,000 cash—as paid-in capital. The annual license fee is $9,000.

Financial privacy is a long-held tradition here. And secrecy laws are closely monitored. When compared to most other centers, the Cayman Islands rate well. If it were not for the government's closed-door policy, this would be a perfect offshore choice.

Hong Kong

Located on China's Southeast coast, Hong Kong is yet another British colony, and one of the best natural harbors in the world. Measuring only 404 square miles, Hong Kong has a population of five million. The colony's capital and main commercial center is Victoria, and jet setters still consider it one of the world's more interesting stop-overs.

The colony is not an actual tax haven but is a complete offshore financial center. A basically conservative banking mentality predominates. And local officials issue offshore licenses only when they are convinced of an individual's (or a corporation's) banking background and expertise.

Hong Kong has an excellent infrastructure. Local banks, as well as legal and accounting services, are outstanding. But, because no tax treaty exists between the United States and Hong Kong, there is a 30-percent withholding tax imposed on all interest payments remitted to local banks.

In short, Hong Kong is a good choice for any large establishment's foreign branch or representative office. But it would be a poor location site for any privately owned offshore bank. Burdensome red tape, a $2-million paid-in-capital requirement, and the government's negative attitude toward nonbankers rule it out for most individual investors.

Mariana Islands

The Marianas are located 400 miles north of Guam and 1,800 miles southeast of Hong Kong. With a resident population of just 15,000, an average year-round temperature of 80 degrees, and evening sunsets that remind visitors of a Gauguin, these Pacific Basin islands are among the most remarkable vacation spots on earth.

The only jurisdiction in the world standing as a self-governing colony of the United States, the Marianas offer international investors the benefits of a unique political environment. For instance, assets housed here are beyond the reach of domestic law but remain as secure as those held on account in any U.S. bank.

Based on offshore banking regulations established in early 1982, the Marianas remain one of the newest offshore centers. Investors can be certain all assets deposited here will be protected by the Federal Deposit Insurance Corporation (FDIC). In addition, the islands have excellent communications systems, a fine offshore banking infrastructure, guaranteed confidentiality, and a nominal $1,000 annual license fee. The paid-in-capital requirement is $10,000.

Overall, the islands' government welcomes foreign investors. Officials have pledged to encourage offshore banking, but they maintain a watchful eye on its development. Local objectives are to increase the influx of foreign capital; gain international recognition by hosting reputable offshore bankers; and enhance the present infrastructure by improving already acceptable professional services and increasing the number of commercial banks operating on the islands.

When compared to all other foreign jurisdictions, the Mariana Islands appear to be the best choice for your offshore bank.

Montserrat

Would you believe another British colony? Montserrat is a small island—just 40 square miles—with a total population of 11,500. It was once a volcanic island, and holds three mountain ranges covered with forest. It is often called the "Emerald Isle," surely because of the lush green that floods every lookout.

Communications between the island and the rest of the world are good. There are adequate local facilities, and an impressive infrastructure supports the island's sizable investment community. No taxes are levied on offshore-banking income, and there are no withholding taxes imposed on interest payments remitted to local banks.

In general, the Montserrat government favors offshore banking, charging each bank an annual license fee of $7,600. The quality of local regulation is quite good. There is a $300,000 requirement for paid-in capital, but it can sometimes be waived or postponed. The island also maintains tight secrecy laws, enjoys a good reputation among domestic bankers, offers comprehensive tax protection, and has no monetary ties to the United States.

In sum, if you are an entrepreneur looking for your first offshore involvement, Montserrat may well be a wise jurisdictional choice.

Netherlands Antilles

Strategically located in the Caribbean Sea, the Netherlands Antilles constitute one of the most important junctions between Europe, North America, and South America. At one point, they are just 40 miles east of Puerto Rico and, at another, only 40 miles off the coast of Venezuela.

Technically, the Netherlands Antilles are a Dutch colony, are fully autonomous in their internal affairs. Direct flights (on a regular basis) make the Antilles, as they are commonly known, a charming getaway for weary U.S. professionals.

At the same time, excellent communications systems keep the jurisdiction in close contact with financial centers all over the world.

Relevant offshore banking regulations are highly regarded within the international banking community. Secrecy laws are stringent. And brass-plate facilities operating from this center enjoy the benefit of a well-nurtured United States-Antilles rapport—while they avoid the dangers of banking within a jurisdiction that maintains monetary ties with this country.

There are no annual fees required from offshore banks established in the Antilles. However, entry requirements are typically burdensome. For instance, each banking license entails $500,000 worth of paid-in capital. Two more major obstacles tend to eliminate the Antilles from most investors' shopping lists. First, the government does not look favorably upon inexperienced bankers. And aside from the general tax-treaty benefits covered in Chapter 6, tax protection is minimal.

Panama

The Republic of Panama is located in the southernmost part of the isthmus linking North and South America. Covering approximately 29,700 square miles, Panama supports a total population of nearly two million. Excellent flight connections are available from the United States and elsewhere, and the country falls within the same time zone as New York City.

Because it is an independent nation, in a politically volatile part of the world, much of the international business community worries about Panama's financial stability. Beyond such concerns, the local government has a poor attitude toward offshore banks owned by nonbankers. To hold potential investors at bay, official policy requires an annual license fee of $4,000. And the country's paid-in-capital requirement is $500,000. Worst of all, Panama relies on extensive monetary ties with the United States. The result is a lack of financial privacy vis-a-vis the IRS and other domestic agencies.

On the positive side, Panama's banking regulations are quite good. The country's financial infrastructure is considered adequate, and there are no taxes levied on offshore-banking income. However, no tax treaty exists between the United States and Panama. So, there are withholding taxes imposed on interest payments remitted to local banks.

On a comparative basis, Panama would seem to be one of the less desirable choices for an offshore bank.

Turks and Caicos

You have probably heard of the Turks and Caicos Islands. Indeed, they have been largely ignored in the rush to open offshore banks in other, more established Caribbean jurisdictions. Yet the Turks and Caicos—located at the southern end of the Bahamas chain—may offer great promise as a future financial center.

Watch these islands carefully and see how their position changes. The islands' lack of international notoriety may eventually prove their greatest appeal. Already, one-on-one relationships (with bankers, accountants, tax lawyers, and government representatives) are an automatic part of banking within this locale. And pristine beaches rolling alongside crystal blue waters make the islands nothing short of gorgeous, tranquil hideaways.

Nonetheless, as things stand today, communications systems are acceptable at best. The banking infrastructure is fair. There is no tax imposed on offshore-banking income, but there is a U.S. withholding tax on interest payments remitted to a Turks and Caicos bank. Local government is less than enthusiastic about expanded banking activity (although the islands did recently pass a strict financial secrecy law).

In the final analysis, the Turks and Caicos would appear to be one of the less desirable selections for today's offshore banker. But watch out for tomorrow.

Vanuatu

Believe it or not, there is a string of 100 islands that receive plentiful rainfall, offer rich soil topped with luxurious flora, and possess dazzling, unspoiled beaches. These are the islands of Vanuatu. Less than 100,000 people live on the tiny islands situated 1,400 miles southwest of Sidney, Australia.

Vanuatu, formerly the New Hebrides, is an independent country. And two connections can transport you from virtually anywhere in the continental United States to this beautiful vacation resort. Vanuatu has publicly supported and encouraged offshore financial activity, which could indicate it is more politically stable than other countries in a similar island position.

The communications systems available in Vanuatu are excellent. The region's infrastructure is exceptional. No taxes are imposed on offshore-banking income. However, there is a U.S. withholding tax on all interest payments made to a Vanuatu bank. (This problem has often been avoided through the use of Netherlands Antilles corporations allowing careful investors to take advantage of attractive tax-treaty provisions.)

The government's attitude toward offshore banks owned by nonbankers is very good. Experts rate the quality of local banking regulation very high. And strong secrecy laws are regularly monitored and secured. The annual license fee for operating a private bank in Vanuatu is only $2,000. The paid-in-capital requirement is $150,000.

On a comparative basis, Vanuatu would appear to be one of today's most attractive offshore banking centers.

In general, I suggest individual investors (and small corporations) consider the Mariana Islands, Montserrat or Vanuatu as an appropriate offshore banking site. All three jurisdictions offer a positive government attitude, realistic but not lax entry requirements, reliable communications systems, ample tax protection, an unblemished banking reputation, and strict measures to assure your financial privacy.

COMPARATIVE ANALYSIS OF OFFSHORE BANKING CENTERS

Country	(1) Political Status	(2) Annual License Fee in U.S. Dollars	(3) Quality of Banking Regulation	(4) Paid-in Capital Requirements in U.S. Dollars	(5) Communications Systems Telephone Telex Mail	(6) Desirability As Vacation Spot	(7) Air Connections from U.S.	(8) Offshore Banking Infrastructure	(9) Taxes on Banking Income	(10) U.S. Withholding Tax on Interest Payments	(11) Government Attitude Toward Offshore Banks Owned by Non-Banks	(12) Banking Secrecy Law
ANGUILLA	British Colony	$ 7,600	Poor	$ 187,500	Poor	Poor	One	Poor	None	Yes	Good	Yes
BAHAMAS	Independent	$ 6,000	Excellent	$1,000,000	Excellent	Excellent	Direct	Excellent	None	Yes	Poor	Yes
BARBADOS	Independent	$13,000	Poor	$1,000,000	Good	Excellent	Direct	Fair	Yes	No	Poor	No
BRITISH VIRGIN ISLANDS	British Colony	$ 4,500	Fair	$ 125,000	Good	Good	One	Fair	Yes	No	Fair	No
CAYMAN ISLANDS	British Colony	$ 9,000	Excellent	$ 500,000	Excellent	Excellent	Direct	Excellent	None	Yes	Poor	Yes
HONG KONG	British Colony	$ 5,000	Excellent	$2,000,000	Excellent	Excellent	One	Good	Yes	Yes	Poor	Yes
NETHERLAND ANTILLES	Dutch Possession	None	Good	$ 500,000	Excellent	Good	Direct	Excellent	Yes	No	Poor	Yes
MARIANA ISLANDS	American Commonwealth	$ 1,000	Excellent	$ 10,000	Excellent	Excellent	One	Excellent	None	No	Excellent	Yes
MONTSERRAT	British Colony	$ 7,600	Good	$ 300,000	Good	Excellent	One	Good	None	No	Good	Yes
PANAMA	Independent	$ 4,000	Good	$ 500,000	Good	Poor	Direct	Good	None	Yes	Poor	Yes
TURKS AND CAICOS	British Colony	$ 7,500	Fair	$ 500,000	Fair	Good	Direct	Poor	None	Yes	Fair	Yes
VANUATU	Independent	$ 2,200	Excellent	$ 150,000	Excellent	Excellent	Two	Excellent	None	Yes	Good	Yes

DATA AS OF: 10/1/82

Earlier, I mentioned the Reagan Administration's Caribbean Aid Plan. The proposal is precisely that—a proposal. But all signals indicate it will be law before the 1984 election. This plan would allow the Internal Revenue Service to break the bank secrecy laws of eight long-established Caribbean tax havens.

A provision within the plan's technical stipulations demands that all countries benefiting from the monetary-aid program cooperate fully with IRS tax investigations involving U.S. citizens. If implemented, the plan will transform Anguilla, the Bahamas, the Cayman Islands, Costa Rica, Montserrat, the Netherland Antilles, Panama, and the Turks and Caicos Islands into monitored extensions of onshore bank sites.

Five of these would appear to be in a no-win situation. Anguilla, Costa Rica, Montserrat, Panama, and the Turks and Caicos have only just begun to develop self-sustaining economies, and their respective unemployment rates are extremely high. Each of these foreign centers has already accepted U.S. aid as well as investment concessions. As a result, they are all dependent on U.S. cooperation for continued economic growth. Given the realities of hard times and their track records for compromise, these countries will probably abandon their tax-haven status in exchange for more U.S. funding. And virtually all offshore businessmen will leave. Few Americans will conduct their affairs in an offshore center providing the IRS with financial information.

But the other three countries—the Bahamas, Caymans, and Netherlands Antilles—have prospered from their tax-haven business. The loss of offshore banking would be devastating to these island governments. My guess is that they will either refuse to cooperate with the IRS, or feign compliance that never bears fruit.

In light of the Caribbean Aid Plan, I would recommend that you first use offshore centers in less controversial areas than the Caribbean. Newer jurisdictions—in the Pacific and even Europe—offer impressive benefits at far less risk. Second, seek professional consultation. An experienced advisor will be able to steer you clear of potentially troublesome offshore locations. Trends change, and the relative desirability of various sites fluctuates. That will always be the case. So, keep on top of things.

Remember my client, Dave Brooks? He finally picked an offshore jurisdiction, and has been extremely happy with the results. I can't tell you what center he chose; he made me promise I wouldn't. I guess he figures that if he worked that hard to make a decision, you should work a little bit yourself . . . .

CHAPTER 8

ON FILE:
OFFSHORE BANKERS

As you are likely to learn for yourself, offshore banking is a world full of doers—people who make things happen. In fact, the thing I like best about the field is its attraction to innovative individuals.

In my opinion, money has the uncanny ability to draw people out of their shells and open them to new possibilities. Every week, I have an opportunity to talk with international investors about their real-life situations. And, whether the end result is a signed contract or just a meeting over coffee, I inevitably walk away with a better sense of the intricacies of personal money management—especially as they apply to offshore banking. I have learned that every client is different. Each one has his own priorities, his own worries, his own ambitions.

My firm—WFI Corp.—has put together close to 200 offshore banks for individuals, small consortiums, and medium-sized companies. With each of these charters and bank licenses has come the chance to meet yet another investor with an entirely new set of problems and priorities. On some level, I like all my clients. But some are very special. Certain people stand out because they taught me new ways of utilizing offshore banks. I remember some just because they were unique—in dress, mannerisms, and in their outlook. True originals. A few I will always associate with their personal stories of triumph over background and financial odds, and others with their ability to improve on a well-heeled birthright.

I hope the ten stories that follow will help illustrate the needs that give rise to offshore banking as well as the resultant benefits. Each one is a tale of creativity and shrewd business instinct. All of them suggest that with forethought and the proper advice an offshore bank facility can be established that meets your financial needs.

So, read carefully. And perhaps between the lines you will learn why I find offshore banking so invigorating.

A Dutch Treat

I was once asked to address a financial conference being held in the Bahamas. My remarks were to center on offshore banking's innumerable tax-protection benefits. Throughout the presentation, there were two gentlemen so persistent with their questioning that I finally suggested we meet afterwards for a drink and some private conversation. They agreed, and the three of us spent a long evening sipping scotch in one of the island's most luxurious hotels. I can still recall the late summer sunset and their intriguing questions.

Both men were Dutch. Paul was an attorney living in California with his wife and son. His associate, Jan, spoke English with a British accent and lived in Amsterdam. They had known each other since childhood and were interested in the possibility of forming an offshore facility to meet their business needs.

Jan owned a large real-estate company based in Holland. International Properties Ltd. sold California land tract property to Dutch nationals and other Europeans looking for a risk-free investment venture. The firm maintained an extensive network of brokers across the Continent, and was considered one of the most successful companies of its kind in Europe. By working together—Jan finding interested European buyers, Paul acquiring the land, recording title, and managing all necessary paperwork here in the United States— the two men had managed to turn a creative idea into an amazingly successful business.

They explained their specific plans for an offshore bank. Both men were eager to avoid the heavy Dutch tax imposed on all company profits, and hoped that a privately owned facility (based, they supposed, in the Caribbean) would allow them to maintain funds offshore and beyond the reach of the Netherlands' government. The idea sounded reasonable, and we pursued it at some length.

Then, as conversation continued, it occurred to me that the bank could also be used as an escrow company. By adding this second element to their plan, I reasoned that Jan and Paul could use their offshore bank facility as an intermediary for the purchase of all California real estate. In the process, they would gain more influence over the written terms and conditions of each escrow and simultaneously impress their clients. After all, who wouldn't be a bit awed by the fact that International Properties' land sales and escrows were handled by an offshore bank? I also noted that as the bank's owners, Jan and Paul would enjoy the use of all escrow funds on reserve in the bank.

They liked the idea and agreed to investigate its possible benefits. We talked until midnight—and over more scotch and sodas than I care to remember. But when I left for the United States two days later, they wanted to meet with me in Los Angeles to finalize details on purchasing a charter and license.

In the end, my two associates decided to purchase the Island Bank and Trust Co., located in the Cayman Islands. The bank's original owner was quite old and had no relations or close associates to handle the details of his offshore venture. He was happy to find a reputable buyer at a good price. And Jan and Paul were glad to acquire an already established bank because it saved them valuable start-up time. As a final feature, their private bank allowed them to take advantage of U.S. tax law. Because all transactions would be handled in the bank's name, profits would fall under the "nonresident" provisions of our domestic tax code and accordingly remain untaxed.

Think Big

Federico Solis is not the sort of man you forget. He lives in an Acapulco Spanish-style villa he designed himself. He originally learned about WFI through a friend of his family, and was only thirty-one when I met him in 1980. He walked into my office one afternoon wearing a beautifully tailored suit, and carrying the most elegant briefcase I've ever seen. "Elephant hide," he remarked. "I had it especially made for myself in Africa."

But behind his elegant persona, Federico is a brillant businessman, the son of a well-respected Mexican industrialist, and, in his own right, worth well over $30 million. Hardly the soft-spoken type, he sat down and explained the workings of what turned out to be a very lucrative offshore venture.

Solis was interested in establishing an offshore bank that would serve as the intermediary for people he called "the big boys," meaning the largest American corporations and the biggest banks in Europe. His idea was completely original, and opened my eyes to an entirely new way of using offshore banks. First, he would garner potential borrowers and then advise certain banks of their interest as a way of attracting sizable lenders. He reasoned that if an offshore facility were able to attract big-name borrowers—for instance, the Fortune 500 companies—it would automatically attract big-name lenders, such as Union Bank of Switzerland, Barclays, and Credit Commercial. He was right, of course. And I found the idea intriguing.

The first step in Fred's plan was to obtain financial mandates from several multinational corporations. With his Swiss-American Bank fully chartered and licensed to do business in Montserrat, he began work. Introducing himself as the Mexican representative for the Swiss-American Bank, he scheduled luncheon appointments with the treasurers of various Fortune 500 companies. After sundry business preliminaries, he would get to the real point: he could offer each treasurer lower borrowing rates than they were finding elsewhere. Needless to say, few doors were closed in his face.

Within ninety days, he had ten letters in hand. Each had been signed by a treasurer, all of them indicating that a major corporation was looking for funds at some specific interest rate. Fred then flew to Europe and approached the leading banks on the Continent. He later told me that he made it a rule never to meet with anyone but an institution's top executive. The results were impressive: virtually every banker committed himself to extending loans—at the rates Fred had quoted to the Fortune 500 corporations.

By using his offshore bank as a broker for the loans, Fred negotiated a small commission on each financial package. With every loan amounting to at least $15 million, his combined commissions were sizable. After just one year of such negotiations, his profits amounted to $4.5 million!

I haven't talked to Fred in almost a year, but I often wonder what brilliant idea he has recently conceived. For a man whose greatest passion is crystal miniatures, he thinks on a grand scale. By taking a simple idea (that is, putting lenders in touch with the right borrowers) and merging it with the basic principles of offshore banking, he has magnified profits beyond the wildest dreams of most investors.

Duran's New Game

I first heard about Louis B. Duran from a former client who suggested that I write and propose a possible offshore involvement. For months, I made efforts to reach him—by letter and phone. But my letters went unanswered and my calls were always received by the same polite but formal secretary who promised only to pass along the message. Then one day I got a call from Duran. He said simply that he would be in Los Angeles for the evening and asked if I might meet with him around 10 in his hotel room. His manner was professional yet strangely secretive. I said that 10 would be fine.

Over coffee in his hotel room, I learned that he was from Nevada and had made his fortune through various gaming and real-estate investments. From the first, I appreciated his candor. He volunteered financial information without blinking an eye, and estimated his net worth to be somewhere in the neighborhood of $4 million.

At that time, he held 51 percent of a company that owned, maintained, and operated 200 video games in the Lake Tahoe area. He was also the director and part owner of a well-known casino in the Reno area, a full-fledged operation with slot machines, 21 games, Keno, poker, roulette, craps, a bar, and restaurant. And, of course, he owned a Nevada gambling license.

Over the years, he had seen Nevada change and grow. As he sat erect in his hotel armchair, gesturing and joking about his business, he seemed utterly at ease with the world of gambling, and rather matter-of-fact about the tremendous wealth he had earned from his involvement with it. But he also confided that he was planning to liquidate his interest in the casino. Meeting with me was part of his plan to find new financial interests.

"Malls," he said, "are the future." Mr. Duran found them fascinating and had already served as a silent investor for two shopping complexes, one of them in Las Vegas. Most recently, he had become involved in a large complex near Carson City.

To make a long story short, he continued to fly in from Nevada—always in the evenings—and we would meet in his hotel room to discuss details of an offshore bank in Vanuatu. We signed the final papers for his offshore bank in the VIP lounge at the Los Angeles International Airport.

The last time we spoke, he said the International Bank of Vanuatu was doing quite well, that he was using it to handle his investment loans, finance new ventures, escape burdensome onshore taxes, and to help him buy a majority interest in three Texas oil wells. He was in the middle of another mall project—this one just outside Denver. And he was thinking about marrying one of the architects involved in the project. Vanuatu, he mentioned, might be a perfect honeymoon hideaway. I wished him the best, wondering if their lives would be spent in secret romantic rendezvous. . . .

At the Club

Darrell Cass Taylor III is the picture of old American aristocracy. The essence of East Coast propriety, he is a dapper and conservative older gentleman. He wears the very finest suits and sweaters imported from England, but I doubt that anything bolder than navy blue has ever graced his patrician shoulders.

Darrell is the chair of several modest-sized banks in upstate New York. Aside from sheepherding these red-carpet institutions, his one great hobby is his men's club. As I understand it, his is no ordinary gentlemen's gym, but a venerated tradition. I suspect that in his old-fashioned way, Darrell sees it as the single refuge from a world gone more than a little haywire. A man of inner sanctums, where hushed voices and thick carpeting comfort the city's "old money," Mr. Taylor likes the quiet ambience of tax havens. An offshore center's serenity and privacy appeal to him.

He called me one day about setting up an offshore bank, and was certain he wanted it based in the Mariana Islands. He had already done a bit of initial legwork, and knew six club members who were ready to form a small investment consortium. Since Darrell was an experienced onshore banker, the offshore enterprise would allow him to capitalize on polished banking expertise.

After all the papers were drawn and duly filed with the proper authorities, he flew off to meet with his new resident agent. I didn't hear from him for a while, but his next call explained a lot about how he had intended to utilize the Mariana bank.

When he returned from the Pacific, Darrell met with just a few more personal friends, and wound up with an eleven-member consortium—made up of fellow club members and personal associates. Their combined deposits amounted to well in excess of $10 million. All of them held certificates of deposit guaranteeing 21-percent interest. Darrell, in turn, was purchasing various money instruments such as T-bills, bankers' acceptances, commercial paper, and other money-market obligations. In this consortium case, interest was never paid. Instead, depositors maintained assets on account and let their money accrue. In the process, they avoided all tax on their earnings and were slowly coming to understand the rules and regulations of international investment.

In the spring of 1982, I was approached through the mail by one of the club members. He is happy with his present arrangement but now sees the universe of opportunity that might open if he himself opened a similar bank and garnered his own depositors.

A Family Affair

In January of 1982, I received a letter from John Mill Howard requesting information on offshore banks. Mr. Howard lived in Western Canada, and wanted to know specifically how he might use an offshore facility to combine personal and business banking. As it turned out, he had organized a small investment company in the early 1960s as a way of managing his family's finances. Through a series of good business decisions and careful reinvestment, he had acquired majority interest in several mining and mineral companies.

I sent him a brochure and general background information. Shortly thereafter, he called to say that his entire family would be in Palm Springs for a few weeks around early February. "Anything to get away from this year's winter," he shuddered. I suggested we make an appointment to discuss his priorities and the possible advantages of moving offshore.

When he arrived for the meeting, he was accompanied by his wife and two grown children—a son and a daughter. Within minutes, it was clear that the Howards were extremely close-knit, and each small decision along the way was tackled through consensus. All four people asked detailed questions and probed until completely satisfied that they'd been answered. In my work I have learned to stay fairly clearheaded even through long meetings. But this one holds first prize for brain-drain. By the time we shook hands and agreed to meet again the following week, I was ready for a hot shower and a couple of aspirin. I had been interrogated by four exceptionally bright people for nearly two hours. But the exhaustion was sweet misery because I knew the Howards would start an offshore bank.

During that second meeting I learned, in more detail, about the family's financial profile. John Mill Howard was a geologist, and served as the president of Pacific Resources Ltd., a mining and mineral-exploration firm operating in Canada and the United States. Pacific was just one part of a larger parent company that held four other mining and mineral-exploration firms.

The Howards were interested in establishing their own off-shore bank as a way of borrowing funds from abroad—namely from West Germany and France. They were confident that further mineral exploration would reap substantial rewards, but needed an immediate influx of capital in order to get the project going. So, the bank's first priority was to target and secure at least $25 million. Simultaneously, the Howards wanted their bank to manage all other family investments, including two well-endowed trusts. At that time, Mr. Howard's personal net worth was $7 million; his wife was worth nearly $3 million; and both the son and daughter claimed a combined worth of $750,000. All four would be equal partners in the bank.

(The Howards wanted an offshore bank to handle very basic financial needs. I tell their story only because it's rare to meet a family that can work so constructively on a joint-investment program.)

Early in 1982—not long after their license had been approved—a series of loans was negotiated with two separate European banks. Pacific Resources had already begun exploration of a mine located in Wyoming. With things pretty much settled on that score, the family was starting to use its bank for other, more sophisticated ventures. Mr. Howard, for instance, has since used the offshore bank facility to purchase a fledgling oil company in Alaska.

Her Own Bank

Four years ago, Debra Ashley was a bookkeeper working in Scottsdale, Arizona. Today, she is the chief executive officer of her own tax and financial-planning firm. She also holds a controlling interest in two other companies: one, a light industrial firm; the other, a publishing house. As Debra tells the story, she went from a net worth of zero to combined assets of over $350,000 in just four years because she watched what her boss did, and figured out ways of doing it better.

Debra worked for the same accountant for nearly nine years, and was earning enough money to support herself and her two children. But she wanted more of a career. So, she worked during the day, and went to school at night. In 1977, she passed the state board examination, and was qualified as a certified public accountant.

She continued on with the same employer until an attractive opportunity presented itself. Following up on a suggestion from her ex-husband, Debra contacted a young accountant based in Phoenix. Janet had only recently earned her CPA license, was eager to find an experienced partner, and liked the idea of working with another woman. It seemed a perfect match, and in August of 1978 Debra packed her professional certificate, her two small children, a self-defrosting refrigerator, and drove off into a brand new life.

When I met her, Debra had spent nearly two years in the professional partnership. She liked Janet, and she liked Phoenix. But she wanted to sophisticate the firm. We talked at some length about offshore banking, and she seemed well aware of its many benefits. Primarily, she was looking for a professional edge over local competitors. She explained to me that the firm was earning a solid reputation in the city, but that two women accountants still faced professional discrimination. She was convinced that if she could offer local residents the services of an offshore bank—especially as a means to legal tax protection—she would position herself to handle the most prestigious clients in Phoenix.

She was right. In 1981, Debra acquired an offshore bank facility in Vanuatu. The entire negotiation took just four months and cost the firm only $25,000. It's been almost two years and Debra is well on her way to becoming a nationally recognized businesswoman. Her Phoenix clients enjoy not only a tax haven where their assets are safe from the IRS but an opportunity to earn handsome interest profits as well.

Debra is a determined person with an innate ability to cut through the babble of everyday conversation and strike deep at the heart of a business matter. No doubt this has contributed to her success. But Debra's achievements also result from her driving need to be special. She was not born into luxury, nor did early adulthood prove a fairy tale of suburban affluence. Yet Debra wanted the best that life could offer. She decided to get it for herself. Owning and operating an offshore bank is her way of saying, "I've made it."

From Lugano with Love

Offshore banking is not only the preoccupation of curious investors and adventuresome entrepreneurs. As Renato Orelli can testify, some of the most experienced bankers in the world have established their own foreign facilities.

Orelli is from Lugano, a small city in Switzerland at the foot of the Alps on the Southern border near Italy. Renato remembers growing up on stories of Swiss banking, and being thrilled by the mystery of secret numbered accounts held by rich exiles and exotic refugees. He also remembers that tall bankers, in their dark suits and homburgs, were among the city's most respected public figures. He liked their stern reserve and imagined the conversations they must have had in large rooms of dark wood and rich red leather. While his friends dreamt of joining the circus, Renato dreamt of taking his place in such a stately room.

Renato's father was a jeweler, and rather well-connected in the Italian sector of Switzerland. Once he realized his son's childhood fantasy was becoming a life's ambition, he did everything he could to help. He financed Renato's university training, first in Basel, and then in Rome. Later, he approached a family friend—a banker living in Toronto—about the possibility of working with Renato for a few years. With the right professional guidance, Orelli was certain his son could master English and, more important, would be exposed to the subtleties of international finance.

In 1961, after three years in Canada, Renato returned to Switzerland. The experience in North America had been a good one, but enough to show him that his banking fantasies were deeply rooted to a life in Lugano. He had focused his ambitions and realized that what he wanted was not just to be a banker, he wanted to be a very special sort of banker. He wanted to provide Old World service, establish close relationships with his clients, and familiarize himself with their investment needs. Well into his late twenties, Renato's goals still centered on those big rooms; for him, banking in Canada and the United States was a little too antiseptic. He preferred Lugano, where bankers were still a bit stern and a source of the city's pride.

Following his father's advice, Renato took his time, and step by step built an impressive Swiss banking career. For six years, he served as the manager of a small bank in Lugano. The position allowed him to build an image of cautious intelligence and calculated initiative. When he left the bank in 1968, he joined four other investors who were forming their own bank. Between them, they established one of the most sophisticated institutions in Switzerland. Within a few years, Finanvest Banca was offering a wide range of ultramodern financial services—all of them delivered in the manner of Old World banking.

When Orelli came to see me three years ago, he was nothing less than an internationally respected banker. He knew almost as much about offshore banking as I did, and saw it as a way to further expand his professional expertise. He was, at that time, involved in several investment ventures and had been appointed the director of six joint stock companies in Switzerland. Although he was a bit evasive about his total financial worth, I am certain his assets topped $3 million.

Specifically, he was eager to establish an offshore bank in association with a few longtime friends. Evidently, they had been involved in a number of past investment opportunities and enjoyed the nature of consortium activity. Renato was clearly in charge of all details. Within a matter of hours, he had decided on a jurisdiction (Netherlands Antilles), a name (Swiss Credit International Bank), and a number-one banking priority (to obtain financing for a textile factory in Shanghai). Within weeks, he had managed to bring together a large group of European investors and had solidified the entire transaction.

Orelli says the offshore experience has proven to be all he had hoped for. As of early 1982, the bank was involved in managing real-estate properties for clients in Europe, Canada, and the United States. Thanks to his expertise, Swiss Credit made a smooth transition into international banking.

The General

In 1976, General Robert M. Shorff suffered a near-fatal heart attack. At the time, he was commanding officer of a Marine Corps base stationed on the East Coast. His doctor's order was plain and simple: leave the Corps. After a thirty-year career with the Armed Forces, he never blinked an eye. He took the order like a trained officer and retired.

Luckily, General Shorff had followed the Marine regimen and, for a fifty-four-year-old man, was in excellent shape. He took life a little easy, got to know his wife for the first time, moved to the West Coast (not far from Camp Pendleton), and decided that it was time he went into business for himself.

By mid-1977, a new venture beckoned. Along with an old friend who once piloted jets for the Air Force, General Shorff formed a mid-sized commercial airline, Air Nevcal. The two men still operate their company mostly out of the Southwest and Mexico. It was in the summer of 1980 that General Shorff arrived in my office. His partner was not with him, but a former military attache was at his side, taking notes and staying noticeably silent throughout the meeting. The general estimated his assets at $1.5 million. And he felt it was time to make a move offshore. He said he wanted to command a financial force that could function internationally.

In addition to Air Nevcal, he was involved in a three-way business partnership. Prime Associates, as the company is called, buys real estate, improves on the properties, and then sells them at a profit. Shorff felt a private offshore bank seemed the next logical step in his personal-investment portfolio.

He had a number of immediate uses in mind. First, he and his partner wanted to establish a second airline—this one to fly routes between the Caribbean and Mexico. They had already contacted interested U.S. investors and had ample capital lined up in Mexico. (In the mid-'50s, General Shorff had commanded a Marine unit assigned to guard the U.S. embassy in Mexico City. Obviously, he had taken full advantage of a long-standing network of professional associates.)

Shorff was also planning to buy a construction company specializing in the grading and paving of commercial and industrial properties. Counting on influential ties to the Defense Department, Shorff was intending to bid on several government construction jobs. For various reasons, tax avoidance among them, he wanted the offshore bank to act as the agent for the purchase of the construction company.

Shorff wound up buying an offshore bank in St. Vincent. I haven't heard from him in some time, and that's a good sign. He's the sort of man who calls only when something needs to be fixed.

The Newport Connection

Again and again, I find that people who start off by opening a foreign bank account inevitably end up reaching the same conclusion: with a solid background in offshore banking, it's better to establish your own offshore bank facility than to deposit money in someone else's. It's a kind of evolution—from initial interest and your first foreign account to a thorough investigation of charter and license purchase.

I once met a fascinating group of five retired couples who had just reached this point of transition. They were all veteran jet setters from one of California's wealthy enclaves: Newport Beach. They had initially met one another through a prestigious social club in the area and had subsequently formed a small investment group to handle their personal money matters. The consortium provided a comfortable environment in which they exchanged information and financial suggestions. As a matter of course, they had dinner once a week, and intermittent phone conversations connected them in a casual but solid way. As I recall, they had named themselves the Newporter Investment Club.

They first approached me after a three-day offshore conference and explained that for almost four years they had been investing as a group—via an established offshore bank in the Bahamas. They were interested in starting their own facility in either the Caribbean or the Pacific islands. We scheduled a meeting for the next day, and en masse, they entered at precisely 2:30.

The afternoon proved an exciting series of discoveries for them. As they learned of the advantages of owning their own offshore bank facility, they became interested in immediate ownership. By 4:00 they had decided to establish a bank in the Caymans. They liked the islands' international reputation. They could afford the license fee. And the idea of vacations in the Caribbean nicely matched their lifestyles.

Once the initial start-up time had passed, my clients put their Island International Bank to good use. All their investment holdings were transferred to the bank. They began to save money almost immediately because, instead of paying a third-party offshore bank a transaction fee or other special service cost, they simply instructed their resident agent to handle all banking matters. Like Mr. Taylor, the Newporters were able to garner deposits from members of their social club, offer attractive interest earnings, and expand their scope of investment opportunity to the international market.

Houston's Best

John Sedgewick had written to me more than once, requesting rather esoteric offshore information. His inquiries always came by mail, and were always specific in nature. He lives in Houston, and while there on a recent business trip, I called him to arrange a one-on-one meeting. He seemed only moderately intrigued, but we scheduled an appointment for the following day.

His firm is headquartered in one of Houston's towering highrises, a handsome, sleek building with cold air blasting through spotless corridors. When I arrived on the 27th floor, John Sedgewick seemed oddly out of place amid the high-tech chrome and glass. He was, at least at that time, an unassuming businessman. He wore a nondescript gray suit, a perfectly plain white shirt, a navy blue tie—neither narrow nor wide, and classic, wing-tip shoes. I had a clear sense that John wore this uniform (or some facsimile) every day.

There was, however, a single extravagance he allowed himself. John maintained a massive and handsomely decorated office suite. He told me during our first meeting that he enjoys the wide-open feel of floor-to-ceiling windows and spartan accessories. His entire staff consisted of just six employees, but a crew of twenty-five could have easily moved in.

As we talked over coffee, I learned that John owned an escrow company and wanted an offshore bank to hold escrows from third parties. As a risk-free source of profit, he would take the assets sitting in escrow and place them in a Merrill Lynch Cash Management Account. I tried to entice him with the many other benefits and profit potential inherent in such a venture. But his mind was made up; this approach seemed the safest and best to him.

He acquired an offshore bank in Montserrat, and continued to implement his plan—without the slightest variation—for quite some time. Then one day, long after he had started the operation, John called me for some advice. He was seriously thinking about buying into a gold bullion company based in

Virginia, and wanted my views on possible utilizations of his offshore bank. We talked for a while and reviewed several options.

A Growing Industry

These ten stories represent just a small percentage of my offshore-banking clients. There are hundreds of others, and they each tell their own tale of ingenuity and profit. Some involve people who have grown up with money and have learned how to work with it. Others center on self-made men and women who have established a new sense of financial security for themselves and their families.

What always strikes me about any case history is that it proves how offshore banking really functions in a person's life. A brass-plate charter and license may seem like just another extravagant purchase or, at best, an exceptionally creative investment. But in fact it's more than that. The move offshore and the commitment to your own private facility will inevitably mark a new phase in your life. Your financial opportunities will expand, and almost without realizing it you will never look at money and how it works in the same way again. Still, I suspect that the most intriguing offshore-banking story has yet to be told. Maybe it's yours.

CHAPTER 9

WHERE YOU CAN BEGIN

If you've diligently reviewed the material covered so far in this book, you are just about ready to decide whether an offshore involvement is right for you. You've learned that your own offshore-bank facility (and to a lesser extent, an offshore account) can reap financial profit, ensure privacy, and protect assets from excessive taxation. Some of you may opt to keep the information in mind, and save it for another time. But for those of you who want to act now, I have written this final chapter.

Whenever an investor talks with me for any real length of time, we wind up discussing the mechanics of moving offshore. Before making a final commitment, even the most enthusiastic clients find it essential to carefully review and understand the options and different ways to use offshore banks. Unfortunately, there is no single way of doing anything. And that includes offshore banking. So, let's review your options and take a critical look at them all.

Customer or Bank Owner?

The benefits of using an offshore bank are profit, privacy and tax protection. As discussed, you can secure all of these benefits by owning your own offshore bank. Tax protection, because of the way in which U.S. laws are structured, can only be gained by owning an offshore bank. Most people think that an offshore or foreign bank account offers tax benefits. That is true, from the foreign point of view, as most offshore centers do not impose tax on the interest paid on bank deposits. Several countries, Switzerland included, impose a withholding tax on interest paid to nonresidents. From the U.S. perspective, you are taxed here even if you have a foreign account, because the U.S. taxes your worldwide income. What many people do, which I do not recommend, is fail to report their foreign bank accounts. This approach assures criminal liability for not complying with the U.S. tax laws.

If your goal is to gain tax benefits, then own an offshore bank, and establish a bank account in the bank's name. That's doing it right.

As mentioned, you can profit or make more money than you are now making on your investment capital by using an offshore bank. Offshore banks can pay substantially higher interest on deposits than U.S. banks. The reason for this is the cost of money to the banks themselves. U.S. banks must allocate a certain portion of their deposits in reserves. These reserves cannot be loaned. Therefore, they are deprived from making money on one's complete deposit. This loss to the bank is translated in the form of lower interest. Besides the cost to U.S. banks connected to maintaining reserves, they are obligated to pay to the Federal Deposit Insurance Corporation (FDIC) a fee to have each account insured. These two extra costs are reflected by as much as two to three percentage points of interest on deposits.

Offshore banks generally pay what's known as the Eurodollar or Asiadollar rate—the Eurodollar for banks maintaining dollar deposits in Europe or the Caribbean and the Asiadollar for dollar deposits maintained in Asia. The Eurodollar rate is quoted daily in the money-rates section of the *Wall Street Journal.*

The services offered by offshore banks vary from bank to bank. In varying degrees they are far better and more personable than services provided by U.S. banks. I recommend that you consider using an offshore bank that has a good reputation and is willing to provide you the investment expertise you need. I strongly recommend the four banks in Bermuda for starters.

If you are interested in being informed of the many programs and opportunities offshore banks offer, I recommend subscribing to my monthly newsletter, the **Private International Moneyletter.** This newsletter offers continuing information and updates on proven ways to increase profits, legally save taxes, and protect your financial transactions in total privacy. To subscribe, write or call WFI Corporation, 357 South Robertson Blvd, Beverly Hills CA 90211, (313) 855-1000.

If you want to take advantage of the full potential of an offshore bank, then I recommend owning your own. If that is your case, then you will be faced with the first decision.

Will you start from scratch and establish your own facility? Or would you prefer to purchase an offshore bank that has already been established?

There are attractive features in each approach. Basically, it's a matter of time and money. How much are you willing to spend in order to begin operating your own bank? And more than that, how much time are you able to devote to the project? Frankly, if you spend time setting up your own offshore bank, you will pay a price in lost opportunity. For one thing, it will take several months of careful (and expensive) research to intelligently decide upon the best offshore center. And even if you feel confident that your jurisdiction choice is sound, many visits overseas will be needed.

To ensure that your bank's legal framework is well-conceived, I would suggest that you work with a reputable attorney based in your preferred offshore center. You should make every effort to maneuver a personal referral. If you don't know anyone who can recommend an offshore attorney, resign yourself to a long period of meticulous research. Always take the time to check professional references because, upon occasion, U.S. investors find themselves faced with a costly legal bill—and no offshore charter or license to show for it. The legal acquisition of an offshore bank is not an extremely complicated process, but it does necessitate specific background knowledge and expertise. The last thing you want to confront is a bottleneck of foreign text, presented by a lawyer incapable of organizing it for you.

Under your guidance, an experienced offshore attorney will begin drafting your bank charter. Know ahead of time that the process is likely to take several weeks. After all, these articles of incorporation and banking bylaws constitute the backbone of your proposed facility. The charter will literally spell out the reasons why you have decided to establish the bank, and it will specify all financial activities to be conducted.

In addition to the lengthy conversations that precede this draft, your lawyer will need to run a check on the bank's name. Far more often than you might think, investors choose a name only to find out that someone else is operating under the same title. If that turns out to be the case, the entire procedure must begin again, but with a new name.

Usually, the host government approves a well-drafted charter. But you must submit it for official review. As with any other bureaucratic operation, this takes time. If your foreign attorney enjoys an impressive network of island contacts, you can expect legal authorization within several weeks. Without that network, the process may take as long as several months.

It is not terribly uncommon for an investor, working on his own, to be sent back to the drawing board. In other words, a foreign government may demand that you recast your entire charter. Or you may be denied an operating license altogether. At that point, you are back at square one, and looking for another offshore center.

Assuming that the government does approve your bank license, you should immediately retain the services of a resident agent. Expect to spend a few weeks and a few thousand dollars in an effort to properly equip your offshore bank facility. You will need a telex machine, a telecopier, phone systems, the services of a small clerical force, and other sundry incidentals. With luck, your offshore attorney will be able to help actualize this initial start-up. If he cannot, you will need to plan another trip to the island and personally undertake the office setup.

Finally, you can begin printing all necessary banking forms. You will need stock certificates, corporate minutes, certificates of deposit, letters of credit, and other corporate and banking documents. Personal associates may be able to suggest a printer. If not, you again face a research phase.

In short, building your own offshore bank facility from the bottom up takes time—typically, six to eight months. In the end, you have an offshore bank structured to all your personal specifications, but the interim process can be a nightmare of long-distance phone calls, certified letters, government red tape, and ultimate rejection. To be fair, I have worked with clients who prefer to take the chance. They have the time and money to spend on each procedure, and actually enjoy the day-by-day developments preceding final authorization and setup.

But more often, offshore investors view their time as if it were money. For them, six to eight months is simply too long a waiting period. They are eager to begin as quickly as possible, with as little complication as possible. If you find yourself in this situation, I would definitely suggest acquiring an offshore bank that's already been established—a "turnkey."

Essentially, turnkey is a shortcut to an offshore-bank purchase and operation. It implies that someone else has done all the preliminary legwork. The charter and license, resident agent, registered office, board of directors, and facility equipment are prearranged and set up for you. One month after deciding to purchase a bank, you are able to begin banking operations.

The Role of a Consultant

In most cases the do-it-yourself approach is fine if you're an experienced professional at setting up tax-haven companies, or if you have the time, money, and wherewithal to put all the pieces together and are willing to risk the possibility of failing.

If it doesn't sound like that approach is for you, seek out a consultant who can help you acquire an offshore bank that's already been established. I've acted as a consultant to over 100 investors and businessmen just for that purpose and would be willing to meet with you to discuss an offshore involvement and help acquire an offshore bank.

My firm, WFI Corp., is unique. We are the only company in the U.S. today that specializes in providing a low-cost program enabling investors to acquire offshore banks within a few days. Our program saves time and money, and ensures a level of offshore efficiency that cannot be guaranteed to those investors wanting to establish a facility from scratch.

Which Offshore Center Is Best for You?

As you know, out of forty-five offshore banking centers around the world, eleven are considered the best for American investors and businessmen. They are:

1. Bahamas
2. Barbados
3. British Virgin Islands
4. Cayman Islands
5. Hong Kong
6. Netherlands Antilles
7. Mariana Islands
8. Montserrat
9. Panama
10. Vanuatu
11. Turks and Caicos

Of these eleven, we can establish an offshore bank for you in any one of these, provided you can meet the jurisdiction's qualifications. These requirements to qualify vary from time to time. In order to be accurate, I suggest a personal consultation to discuss how the requirements would apply to you and if the country suits your needs.

From time to time I select a country out of the eleven and preestablish an offshore bank. I call these "turnkey" situations because when you ask us to provide you with a bank, we deliver it ready-to-operate with no further setup work needed. Our program removes all of the risk and legwork of setting up an offshore bank on your own.

Typically, our program is offered from an up-to-date off-shore bank offering memorandum. Here are some excerpts from our offering memorandum, where the offshore bank is established in the "Freedom Islands," a mythical place to describe the best country for your own particular needs and situation.

Background

Again, let's assume that for your purposes the Freedom Islands are the best offshore center for your offshore bank. Our first step is to lay out the charter and negotiate with the government of the Freedom Islands for an offshore bank upon application made by WFI Corp. We apply for the charter in WFI's name, because we have already established a working relationship with the government, and we are certain a charter will be issued to WFI. Once established, we hire a resident agent, locate a registered office and tie this arrangement down with an agreement. We then make certain that the bank can be operated in accordance with your needs and wishes. At any one time, it is likely that we already have one such bank already established, with arrangements secured—ready for immediate operation.

The Value of WFI's Program

Value No. 1: No Previous Banking Experience Is Required.

The laws of the Freedom Islands will not require that any one particular person associated with the bank have prior banking experience. Unless, of course, as indicated in Chapter 7, several jurisdictions (such as the Bahamas, and Cayman Islands) make previous banking experience mandatory. The resident agent—who has already been selected by WFI—has more than adequate expertise and will be able to work successfully under the general directions of the bank's shareholders.

Value No. 2: A Turnkey Situation.

Since the bank's charter has already been issued, its license granted, agreements negotiated, and forms printed, this facility is ready to commence business. Just one prerequisite remains at issue: the Freedoms' government must find the new owners acceptable banking candidates. This official formality is likely to involve three to four weeks of paperwork.

Value No. 3: All Legwork Has Been Eliminated.

The tedious and burdensome steps needed to secure an offshore bank's charter and license have already been taken. WFI executives have made several trips to the Freedoms, and the firm has established a network of island contacts that will prove helpful to the bank's ultimate owner.

Value No. 4: A Substantial Cost Savings.

When you attempt to establish an offshore bank on your own, you risk learning (the hard way) that such a process calls for specialized expertise. Without the appropriate background, costly mistakes are made. Several WFI clients have come for advice only after spending more than $100,000 in the fruitless attempt to set up a facility on their own. By committing your resources to a turnkey acquisition, your costs remain fixed and determinable.

Value No. 5: Now Is an Opportune Time.

In most cases the government will be cautious and not easily establish a bank for unknowns. Island officials are extremely cautious, and seek to ensure that only the most reputable investors retain an offshore banking license. WFI's current offering comes at a most opportune time, and ensures access into one of the most reputable of all offshore jurisdictions.

Value No. 6: Postpurchase Support Services Are Offered.

WFI maintains an ongoing rapport with the vast majority of its clients. Although the firm is not involved in the management or operation of any facility, it provides a valuable support to bank owners in the form of business development techniques and ideas, regular seminars, and other information services. Most important, WFI continues to encourage the Freedom government to foster favorable terms and conditions for the operation of offshore facilities. Therefore, as an island banker, you are assured of regularly updated information.

Value No. 7: Comprehensive Powers Currently Available.

At this time, no special license is required to operate a trading company or trust company within the Freedoms, unless you have selected one of the centers that restrict banks from conducting those activities. Investors are not likely to find similar freedom offered by other jurisdictions. The Freedom government may, at some future date, require such a license—but only from new offshore bankers.

Value No. 8: An Appealing Bank Name.

WFI has already selected a bank name it believes will nurture an image of distinction and financial credibility. This name will not mislead or confuse the public. WFI feels that the chosen name will attract depositors and extended service customers.

Value No. 9: An Attractive Purchase Price.

WFI has been careful not to price itself out of the market. The firm has investigated the cost involved in establishing a Freedom bank. We can guarantee clients that our acquisition price is lower than the total cost of establishing an identical institution from scratch.

Value No. 10: The Benefit of Know-How and Technology.

The professional background and experience that WFI can offer its clients is truly inestimable. The firm clearly understands the legal ramifications—both foreign and domestic—that impact upon the use of any offshore facility.

This bank's charter, banking forms, and trained resident agent all reflect a silent corporate technology that comes from WFI personnel.

Description of What You Get from WFI Documentation

Appropriate documentation is, by far, the most complicated aspect of bank acquisition. Essentially, it involves six key documents that form the basis for the bank:

- The Articles of Incorporation and Bylaws
- The Corporate Charter
- The Certificate of Incorporation
- The Banking License
- The Minutes of the First Meeting
- The Share Certificates

(A) The Articles of Incorporation and Bylaws are made up of the articles of incorporation, the bylaws, and an affidavit of incorporation. These three documents are available for review at the office of WFI Corp.

(B) The Corporate Charter is a legal document signed by the governor of the Freedom Islands. It stipulates that the bank is a body corporate, and has had its articles of incorporation and bylaws reviewed and approved. It also proclaims that the bank has been granted a charter to engage in specific banking transactions within the Freedom Islands.

(C) The Certificate of Incorporation is obtained through the Registrar of Corporations. It is a legal document stating that the articles of incorporation have been duly filed and found to be in accordance with the laws of the Freedom Islands. In essence, it constitutes conclusive proof that the bank has been duly incorporated and legally formed.

(D) The Banking License is signed by the head of the banking department for the Freedom Islands. It indicates that the bank is in compliance with all existing municipal ordinances, falls under all other applicable laws in appendices, and is licensed to engage in the business of offshore banking. The license is valid for one year and may be renewed—provided the head of the banking department for the Freedom Islands has received the bank's semiannual report for its condition and, prior to the expiration of its license, has filed an annual report of its financial condition along with payment of the license fee.

(E) The Minutes of the First Meeting are drafted after incorporators and subscribers meet to finalize all necessary bank forms at the offices of WFI. Individuals attending this meeting are named incorporators and subscribers in the bank's articles and bylaws.

At the meeting, the articles of incorporation and bylaws are read, article by article, and unanimously adopted. Such a reading ensures that they are made a permanent entry in the bank's minute book. The initial directors and officers are elected; the resident agent and office service company are designated; the authorization of payment of the initial fee is made; the minute book is designated as the official book for custody of the bank's records; the directors are given the power to issue stock; the share certificates are approved; the issuance of the shares is approved and finalized; and approval of all banking forms is formalized.

(F) Share Certificates constitute conclusive proof that the shareholders do in fact retain interest in the bank. Freedom law requires that all shares be issued to three separate shareholders, and that such shares be maintained by them. For this reason, three separate shareholders must be officially designated.

The Registered Office, Resident Agents and Management Services Agreement

If the Freedom bank intends to operate with any degree of success, its owners must be able to depend on a resident agent, or on a specified manager situated in the Freedom Islands. This bank employee must be capable of executing all owner instructions with extreme precision and 100 percent accuracy. Anything less could result in substantial loss—to the bank's customers and owners. Cognizant of this need, WFI has chosen the Freedom International Trust Co. (FITCO) to function as a foreign representative for the bank's ultimate owner. Again for the purpose of illustration, we have identified the Freedom Islands best management firm as "FITCO." FITCO's extensive banking experience, coupled with ongoing advice and support from WFI, ensures a sophisticated management service organization.

A formal relationship between the offshore bank and FITCO is entered into and adopted at the time of incorporation. Such an agreement has been prenegotiated by WFI to provide the bank's owner with a necessary assurance: his Freedom bank will be legally maintained in an environment that offers efficient management service.

Furthermore, the agreement covers two essential offshore banking features. First, it assures that in compliance with island regulation, the facility will maintain a registered office and resident agent. Second, it guarantees that management services will be available to the bank whenever necessary.

Exclusive Use of Professional Offshore Bank Management Services

To illustrate the everyday advantage of working with FITCO, let's review just a partial list of the company's management services:

- To provide officers, nominee directors, or nominee shareholders upon special request or approval.

- To act as a registered transfer agent for the bank's shares.

- To act as trustee or executor of wills or estates.

- To act as custodian of records, documents, minutes, books, ledgers, files, journals, securities, and negotiable instruments.

- To provide the use of FITCO's telex, telephone, telecopier, and other office equipment.

- To draft and process all agreements made between the bank and creditors (i.e., letters of credit, and international certificates of deposit).

- To execute and/or process all orders and instructions for the purchase or sale of securities, commodities, real estate, bullion, coins, options, bank obligations, T-bills, mutual funds, etc.

- To administer all consolidation activity (i.e., import/export trading, deposit-taking systems, preprogrammed disbursements or remittances, and monthly loan payments).

Banking Forms

Banking forms are an important element in the success or failure of any offshore banking venture. For this reason, WFI has customized and prepared exclusive forms for this particular bank offering. They are colorful and attractive, and conform to all international rules and regulations. They include ten serialized letters of credit and ten serialized international certificates of deposit.

Postpurchase Support

The purchase of an offshore bank is for many people a major undertaking. And as such, it brings with it some apprehension and legitimate concern. To help alleviate this anxiety,

WFI has committed itself to provide clients with continuous postpurchase support. Specifically, we offer:

- Access to books, articles, and newsletters dealing with offshore banking, international tax planning, and tax havens.

- Information and recommendations on new business ideas that can influence business building, tax savings, and the attainment of maximum privacy.

- Invitations to all WFI's seminars and conferences, where participants are exposed to the most cost-effective methods of offshore maintenance.

Access to Precedents

There is little case law to limit the parameters of offshore banking. And little upon which to guard against mistakes. Successful investors typically remain silent with regard to their experiences because they fear an infringement on offshore benefits. To help prospective bankers, WFI maintains an excellent rapport with experienced international investors. As a result, the firm can offer a realistic assessment of various banking procedures. Successful precedent is translated into information that could never be purchased elsewhere—at any price.

Political Influence

In most cases WFI will have already established a number of offshore banks in the Freedom Islands. Because of this WFI can pull together the resources of the banks established there that may be used to promote new legislation and other regulatory changes that would benefit potential investors.

The Credibility of the Offshore Bank and Its Relationship in the International Banking Community

Although the documentation section was extensive, it should offer a bird's-eye view of the inner workings of offshore banking within the Freedom Islands. All documents outlined above guarantee our freedom, offering equal legal status to offshore banks operating out of the Bahamas, Cayman Islands, Switzerland, or United Kingdom.

Because the Freedom Islands are technically considered a sovereign jurisdiction, their license and charter are viewed as authentic and credible in every international center—including the United States. Provided that corporate formalities are observed, documentation issued by any of the islands' banks has legal authority and as much weight as identical documentation issued by any other financial facility. WFI's bank offering has been organized in an orderly and logical manner. As a result, corporate continuity can be systematically traced to the facility's new owners. Upon purchase, a special meeting of the incorporators and subscribers will be held, at which time all bank shares will be transferred. The directors will be designated and, if necessary, agents will be appointed. New bank accounts will be authorized, and signing authorization will be recorded in the minutes.

It is a simple fact of international finance that offshore banks greatly rely on paperwork. Only precise and well-phrased documentation can assert their authority. For this reason, WFI has been extremely careful to ensure that the offered bank is duly recorded to new owners. Had the initial work been poorly handled or submitted in an incomplete fashion, the IRS or other state banking departments might have targeted the facility for review. Potential buyers can rest assured that the offering is presented as a valid financial institution.

How the Offshore Bank May Be Acquired

With a thorough understanding of this background documentation and setup, you are prepared to purchase the turnkey offering. The process of actual acquisition involves four essential steps.

Step No. 1: Standards of Ownership.

The government of the Freedom Islands will be concerned that WFI's offshore bank offering not fall into the wrong hands or be intentionally abused. Official concern stems largely from the need to maintain an unblemished reputation within the international financial community, and has led to an island policy regarding standards for ownership. These standards are meant to protect all present and future owners, and to safeguard the Freedoms' reputation. Specifically:

- The new shareholders must present to WFI Corp. conclusive proof that their net worth (exclusive of home furnishings and automobiles) can satisfy the Freedom government's minimum-net-worth of bank-owner requirement.

- The owners or shareholders must be able to substantiate good character and a reputation for honesty in all financial dealings.

- The new owners and/or shareholders must be able to demonstrate to WFI Corp. that they have in mind a legitimate use for the bank.

Step No. 2: Ownership Transfer.

The mechanics of ownership transfer involve just two steps. First, the new owners and shareholders must prove to WFI Corp. (in writing) that they are acceptable bank owners. This prerequisite would best be met through the firm's purchase agreement. Second, a physical transfer of shares—from the subscribers to the new shareholders—must be actualized. Only after the shares have been appropriately transferred can FIT-CO file a report with the Freedom Island government stating that the bank has changed owners. This report must be accompanied by a background investigation report—which has already been prepared by WFI. With a final island authorization and payment of the bank's purchase price, the new owner can take legal custody of the facility.

Step No. 3: Bank Availability.

The availability of the bank described in this offering depends entirely upon demand. As stated, WFI as a matter of business practice maintains on hand an offshore bank ready to operate in the jurisdiction it belives to be the best.

Typically, WFI incorporates and licenses one bank each month—with no certainty that another bank will be incorporated and licensed in the same jurisdiction. Therefore, if you are a prospective buyer, you should certainly contact the firm by phone before planning to acquire the specific facility outlined above. At that time, you will be informed of all relevant developments and possible alterations in the offering. Chances are, you will want to schedule a personal meeting in Los Angeles to discuss the finer points of any bank purchase.

Step No. 4: Orientation Meeting.

A prearranged and professionally-structured orientation meeting with WFI executives can provide you with a great deal of general information. In most cases, the few days spent in private consultation will facilitate your final determination regarding purchase. Offshore banking is not for everyone. Better to invest now in the information that will guide you toward a responsible decision than to find yourself thousands of dollars into an offshore venture that does not meet your personal portfolio needs.

Before the meeting, identify general topics that you want pursued. And be ready to ask any specific questions that impact on your personal situation. Remember, WFI—like other offshore management firms—is a service-oriented corporation. Our job is to help you meet your needs. We can do that best if you intelligently lay out your present financial situation and indicate areas of personal concern.

You may wish to study and discuss client histories that match your present financial position. It can help a great deal to learn that someone in a predicament much like your own purchased an offshore bank. And lived to cherish the decision. If you think it would be useful, ask about the firm's videotape seminars. It is also possible to review (on a page-by-page basis) the actual offering memorandum outlined above.

Members of my staff are likely to make specific recommendations for the corporate organization and structure of your prospective offshore facility. Their suggestions may include diversification into other jurisdictions or perhaps the use of an intermediary corporation in the Netherlands Antilles. The point is, we are here to meet your needs. Let us know what you require and we will be most happy to provide you with all the information you can handle.

Wrapping Things Up

The object of this book has been to introduce you to the exciting and profitable world of offshore banking. But between the pages and invisibly written under each line has been my own unbridled enthusiasm. Offshore banking has been a good part of my life for almost a decade. I like its challenge. I appreciate the universe of opportunity it offers assertive investors. And I enjoy its unique ability to introduce me to many of the world's most fascinating people.

I sincerely believe that there are those who in their time cross new frontiers. They swallow deep, and jump headfirst into the challenge of a new opportunity. Offshore banking is the frontier of the '80s. It is to personal investment what the microchip is to high technology. It forms the basis of an entirely new and efficient way of doing things. It is for tomorrow's investors today. If such concepts excite you and provoke flights of financial fancy, I'll probably be meeting you one of these days.

APPENDIX A

BAHAMAS

Allied Bank International
Allied Bank and Trust Company (Bahamas) Ltd.
Artoc Bank and Trust Ltd.
Banco Ambrosiano Overseas Ltd.
Bank for Credit and Foreign Commerce (Overseas) Ltd.
Bank of International Credit Ltd.
Bank Leu International Ltd.
Bank of Montreal International Ltd.
Bank of Nova Scotia International Ltd.
BankAmerica International
BankAmerica Trust and Banking Corp. (Bahamas) Ltd.
Bastogi International Ltd.
Charterhouse Japhet Bank and Trust International Ltd.
Chase Manhattan Bank, NA
Chase Manhattan Trust Corporation Ltd.
Credit Suisse (Bahamas) Ltd.
Credit Suisse (Swiss Credit Bank)
Equator Bank Ltd.
First National Bank of Boston
First Pennsylvania Bank NA (Nassau Branch)
Handelsbank NW (Overseas) Ltd.
Interamerican Bank Corporation SA
Interfin Bahamas Ltd.
Intermex International Bank Ltd.
Lloyds Bank International (Bahamas) Ltd.
Royal Bank of Canada International Ltd.
RoyWest Banking Corporation Ltd.
RoyWest Trust Corporation (Bahamas) Ltd.
SFE Bank and Trust (Bahamas) Ltd.
SFE Banking Corporation Ltd.

Swiss Bank Corporation (Overseas) Ltd.
Wardley International Bank Ltd.
Wardley Ltd.

BRITISH VIRGIN ISLANDS

Bank of Nova Scotia
Barclays Bank
Chase Manhattan Bank
Commercial Bank of Tortola
Scotiabank
Virgin Islands National Bank

CAYMAN ISLANDS

Altajir Bank
Arawak Trust Company (Cayman) Ltd.
Baer-American Banking Corporation (opening shortly)
Banco de Brasil SA
BankAmerica Trust & Banking Corporation (Cayman) Ltd.
Bank Intercontinental Ltd.
Bank of Credit & Commerce International (Overseas) Ltd.
*Bank of Nova Scotia
Bank of Nova Scotia Trust Company (Cayman) Ltd.
*Barclays Bank International Ltd.
Barclays Finance Corporation of the Cayman Islands
Bentleys Bank Ltd.
Butterfields Bank & Trust Company Ltd.
*Canadian Imperial Bank of Commerce
Canadian Imperial Bank of Commerce Trust Company
    (Cayman) Ltd.
Cayman International Trust Company Ltd.
*Cayman National Bank & Trust Company Ltd.
Cayman Overseas Bank & Trust Company Ltd.
Discount Bank (Overseas) Ltd.

Dow Banking (Overseas) Ltd.
First Cayman Bank Ltd.
First Cayman Trust Company Ltd.
First Home Savings & Loans (Cayman) Ltd.
First Pennsylvania Overseas Development Company
    (Cayman) Ltd.
Guinness Mahon Cayman Trust Ltd.
Intercontinental Bank & Trust Company
LBI Bank & Trust Company (Cayman) Ltd.
Multi-Banking Corporation (Overseas) Ltd.
Northwest International Bank & Trust Company
*Royal Bank of Canada
Royal Bank of Canada International Ltd.
RoyWest Trust Corporation (Cayman) Ltd.
J. Henry Schroder Bank & Trust Company
Swiss Bank & Trust Corporation Ltd.
United Bank International
Washington International Bank & Trust Ltd.

Licensed banks and trust companies operating through agents

Aall Trust & Banking Corporation Ltd.
Aktieselskabet Varde Bank
Alamo National Bank
Algemene Bank Nederland NV
Allied Irish Banks Ltd.
American Commerce Bank
American Deposit Trust Company
American Express International Banking Corporation
American National Bank and Trust Company of Chicago
American National Bank of Austin
Americapital International Bank
Andelsbanken a/s Danebank

Arab Solidarity Bank
Arabian Express Bank Ltd.
Arc Trust Company Ltd.
Argentine Banking Corporation
Arizona Bank
Armeria Trust Corporation Ltd.
Arteco Trust Company Ltd.
A/S Midtbank
A/S Vendelbobanken
Atlantis Bank Ltd.
Australia and New Zealand Banking Group Ltd.
Baerbank (Overseas) Ltd.
Bai Bank (Cayman) Ltd.
Banco Ambrosiano Overseas Ltd.
Banco de America Central
Banco de Bilbao
Banco de Bogota Trust Company
Banco de Colombia Ltd.
Banco de Credito Nacional SA
Banco de la Nacion Argentina
Banco de la Provincia de Buenos Aires
Banco di Roma (Caribbean) Company Ltd.
Banco do Commercio et Industrie de Sao Paulo SA
Banco do Estado de Sao Paulo SA
Banco Economico SA
Banco Financiero del Caribe
Banco Hispano American
Banco International Finance Ltd.
Banco International SA-Mexico
Banco Itau SA
Bancomer SA
Banco Mercantil de Sao Paulo SA
Banco Mexicano Somex SA
BancOhio National Bank

Banco Noroeste do Estado de Sao Paulo SA
Banco Portugues do Atlantico
Banco Real SA
Banco Totta & Acores
Bank Urquijo SA
Bank for Credit and Foreign Commerce (Cayman) Ltd.
Bank fur Gemeinwirtschaft Aktiengesellschaft
Bank Hapoalim BM
Bank Hapoalim (Cayman) Ltd.
Bank Leumi Le Israel BM
Bank Leumi Trust Company of New York
Bank of America National Trust and Savings Association
Bank of Boston International
Bank of British Columbia
Bank of India
Bank of Ireland
Bank of Montreal Trust Corporation Cayman Ltd.
Bank of New South Wales
Bank of New York
Bank of Oklahoma NA
Bank of the South NA
Bank of the Third World
Bank of Tokyo Ltd.
Bank of Tokyo Trust Company (Cayman) Ltd.
Bank of Virginia (Grand Cayman) Ltd.
Bank One of Columbus NA
Bank Von Ernst Trust Company Ltd.
Bankers Trust (Cayman) International Ltd.
Banque Commerciale (Cayman) Ltd.
Banque de l'Indochine et de Suez
Banque de l'Union Europeenne
Banque de Paris et des Pays-Bas
Banque Francaise du Commerce Exterieur
Banque Nationale de Paris

Banque Scandinave (Overseas) Ltd.
Barclays Bank of California
Baring Brothers Asia Ltd.
Bayerische Hypotheken-und Wechsel-Bank
BCCI Finance International Ltd.
BEG Bank (Cayman Island) Ltd.
Berliner Handels-und Frankfurter Bank
BIPA Bank
Birmingham Trust National Bank
BNS International (Hong Kong) Ltd.
Boatmen's National Bank of St. Louis
Bolivar International Merchant Bank
Bornholmerbanken Aktieselskab
Brasilian American Merchant Bank
Brown Brothers Harriman & Company
Cabaco Ltd.
Caisse Nationale de Credit Agricole
Cambridge Bank & Trust Company Ltd.
Canada International (Cayman) Ltd.
Capital National Bank
Caribbean Bank (Cayman) Ltd.
Cayman Trust Bank Ltd.
Central American Exchange Bank
Central National Bank in Chicago
Central Penn National Bank
Churchill Marine Bank & Trust Ltd.
Chase Manhattan Bank
Chase Manhattan Trust Cayman Ltd.
Citibank NA
Citicorp Banking Corporation
Cititrust (Cayman) Ltd.
Citizens and Southern National Bank of SC
Citizens Fidelity Bank & Trust Company

City National Bank of Detroit
Clariden Bank and Trust (Cayman) Ltd.
Colonial Bank
Commerce Bank of Kansas City NA
Commerce Union Bank
Commercial Bank of Australia Ltd.
Commercial Banking Company of Sydney Ltd.
Commercial Banking Corporation
Commercial Security Bank
Commerzbank Aktiengesellschaft
Commonwealth Trading Bank of Australia
Connecticut National Bank
Continental Bank Ltd.
Continental Investment Bank
Continental National Bank of Fort Worth
Copenhagen Handelsbank A/S (Aktieselskabet Kjobenhavns
   Handelsbank)
Cowrie Ltd.
Credit and Finance Corporation Ltd.
Credit Commercial de France
Credit Industriel et Commercial SA
Credit Lyonnais
Credito Italiano
Crocker International Trust Company (Cayman) Ltd.
Crocker National Bank
Daiwa Bank Trust Company
December Trust Company Ltd.
Den Danske af 1871 Aktieselskab
Den Danske Provinsbank A/S
Denton Bank and Trust Corporation
Deposit Guaranty National Bank
The Detroit Bank and Trust Company
Deutsche Bank Aktiengesellschaft

Deutsche Genossenschaftsbank
Deutsche Girozentrale Overseas Ltd.
Dresdner Bank Aktiengesellschaft
Egnsbank Nord A/S
Equitable Bank and Trust Company Ltd.
Euro Bank Corporation
Eurocredit Bank (Cayman)
European-American Bank and Trust Company
Eurotrade Invest Bank and Trust Corporation
Faellesbanken for Danmarks Sparekasser Aktieselskab
Ferrier Lullin Cayman Bank & Trust
Finacorp Bank
Financial and Investment Services for Asia Ltd.
Finansbanken (International) Ltd.
First American National Bank of Nashville
First Bank
First Chicago Trust Company (Cayman) Ltd.
First European International Bank
First International Bank in Houston, NA
First International Bank of Israel Limited
First National Bank and Trust Company of Oklahoma City
First National Bank in Dallas
First National Bank of Atlanta
First National Bank of Birmingham
First National Bank of Chicago
First National Bank of Commerce
First National Bank of Denver
First National Bank of Greater Miami
First National Bank of Louisville
First National Bank of Maryland
First National Bank of Minneapolis
First National Bank of Oregon
First National Bank of New Jersey

First Overseas Trading Bank (Cayman) Ltd.
Flagship National Bank of Miami
Foreign Trade Bank Ltd.
Fort Worth National Bank
Fuji Bank and Trust Company
Gefinor Bank Ltd.
General Banking Corporation
Georgetown Trust Company
Girard Bank
Gulf Banking and Trust Corporation Ltd.
Habib Bank Zurich (International) Ltd.
Haversine Trust Company Ltd.
Hellerup Bank A/S
Hentsch & Co. International
Hessische Landesbank—Girozentrale
Hibernia National Bank in New Orleans
Huntington National Bank
Hydrocarbons Bank Ltd.
Industrial National Bank of Rhode Island
Industrial Valley Bank & Trust Company
Interlat Bank Ltd.
International Bank of Finance
International Credit and Investment Company (Overseas) Ltd.
International Credit Bank and Trust Company Ltd.
International Mercantile Bank Ltd.
International Resources and Finance Bank (Overseas) Ltd.
Iowa-Des Moines National Bank
Irving Bank of Chicago International Subsidiary Ltd.
Irving Trust Company
Irving Trust Company International/Miami
Israel Discount Bank Ltd.
Israel Discount Bank of New York
Jyske Bank A/S
Kredietbank NV

Kynast Banking Ltd.
La Salle National Bank
Leumi Cayman Finance and Trust Corporation
Lincoln First Bank NA
M & G (Cayman) Ltd.
M & I Marshall & Ilsley Bank
Magellan Bank Ltd.
The Mathilde Trust Company Ltd.
Mellon Bank NA
Mercantile National Bank at Dallas
Mercantile Trust Company National Association
Mercator Bank Ltd.
Merchants Continental Bank Ltd.
Midlantic National Bank
Minden Trust (Cayman) Ltd.
Mitsubishi International Finance Ltd.
Mitsui Finance Asia Ltd.
Morgan Guaranty International Bank (Cayman) Ltd.
Multibanco Comermex SA
Nagrafin Bank Ltd.
The National Bank of Australasia Ltd.
National Bank of Commerce of Dallas
National Central Bank
National City Bank of Minneapolis
Nederlandsche Middenstandsbank NV
New Jersey Bank (National Association)
New Jersey National Bank
Nordic American Banking Corporation
North Carolina National Bank
Northern Trust Company
Northwestern Bank
Old Kent Bank and Trust Company
Orion Caribbean Ltd.

Oryx Merchant Bank Ltd.
Overseas Investment Bank Ltd.
Pacific Bank Ltd.
Pacific National Bank of Washington
Pariente International Bank
Pelikan Bank
Power Bank and Trust Company
Privaco Trust Company Ltd.
Privatbanken A/S
Rainier National Bank
Ralli Bank & Trust Company (Cayman) Ltd.
Real Bank & Trust Company
Republic National Bank of New York
Rhode Island Hospital Trust National Bank
Richard Daus & Co. Bank and Trust Ltd.
Santo Spirito Trust Company Ltd.
J. Henry Schroder Banking Corporation
Schroder Cayman Bank and Trust Company Ltd.
Sears Bank and Trust Company
Shepard Bank
Sjaellandske Bank A/S
Societe Bancaire Barclays (Overseas) Ltd.
Societe Generale pour Favoriser le Developpement du
    Commerce et l'Industrie en France
Solandra Bank and Trust Corporation Ltd.
South Atlantic Bank Ltd.
South Carolina National Bank
Sparekassen SDS
Sparekassen Sydjylland
State Bank of India
State National Bank of Connecticut
State Street Bank and Trust Company
Sumitomo Finance (Asia) Ltd.
Sun Bank NA

Svendborg Bank Aktieselskab
Swiss Bank Corporation
Swiss Investment and Commerce Bank
Swiss Italian Banking Corporation Ltd.
Sydbank A/S
Third National Bank in Nashville
Tokai Asia Ltd.
Towerbank Ltd.
Trafalgar Trust Company Ltd.
Transatlantic Trust Corporation
Trust Company Bank
UBAF Arab American Bank
Underwriters Bank (Overseas) Ltd.
Unibanco—Uniao de Bancos Brasileiros SA
Union Bank of Bavaria (Bayerische Vereinsbank)
Union Bank of Switzerland
Union Planters National Bank of Memphis
Union Trust Company of Maryland
United American Bank in Knoxville
United Bank of Arizona
United Jersey Bank
United Mizrahi Bank Ltd.
United States Trust Company of New York
United States Trust Company of New York
　(Grand Cayman) Ltd.
United Trust Overseas Bank Ltd.
United Virginia Bank
Venecredit International Banking Ltd.
Wachovia Bank and Trust Company NA
Wells Fargo Bank NA
Westdeutsche Landesbank Girozentrale
Winters National Bank and Trust Company of Dayton
World Shipping Development Bank

Worldwide Commercial Bank Ltd.
Zions First National Bank

*These banks are members of the Cayman Islands Bankers Clearing Systems.

HONG KONG

Algemene Bank Nederland NV
American Express International Banking Corporation
Banco di Roma
Bangkok Bank Ltd.
Bank Melli Iran
Bank Negara Indonesia 1946
Bank of America National Trust and Savings Association
Bank of Canton Ltd.
Bank of China
Bank of Communications
Bank of East Asia Ltd.
Bank of India
Bank of Montreal
Bank of Nova Scotia
Bank of Scotland
Bank of Seoul and Trust Company
Bank of Tokyo Ltd.
Banque Belge pour l'Etranger SA
Banque de Paris et des Pays-Bas
Banque Nationale de Paris
Banque Worms
Barclays Bank International Ltd.
Canadian Imperial Bank of Commerce
Chan Man Cheong Finance Company
Chartered Bank
Chase Manhattan Bank NA

Chekiang First Bank Ltd.
Chemical Bank
China and South Sea Bank Ltd.
China State Bank Ltd.
Chiyu Banking Corporation Ltd.
Chung Khiaw Bank Ltd.
Citibank, NA
Commercial Bank of Hong Kong Ltd.
Commerzbank AG
Credit Lyonnais
Credit Suisse
Crocker National Bank
Dah Sing Bank Ltd.
Deutsche Bank AG
DG Bank Deutsche Genossenschaftsbank
Dresdner Bank AG
Equitable Banking Corporation
European Asian Bank
Far East Bank Ltd.
First Interstate Bank of California
First National Bank of Boston
First National Bank of Chicago
Four Seas Communications Bank Ltd.
Fuji Bank Ltd.
Grindlays Dao Heng Bank Ltd.
Hang Lung Bank Limited
Hang Seng Bank Ltd.
Hanil Bank Ltd.
Hongkong Industrial Commercial Bank Ltd.
Hong Kong Metropolitan Bank Ltd.
Hongkong and Shanghai Banking Corporation
Hongkong Chinese Bank Ltd.
Hong Nin Bank Ltd.
Hua Chiao Commercial Bank Ltd.

Indian Overseas Bank
Industrial Bank of Japan Ltd.
Ka Wah Bank Ltd.
Kincheng Banking Corporation
Korea Exchange Bank
Kwangtung Provincial Bank
Kwong On Bank Ltd.
Lee Shing
Liu Chong Hing Bank Ltd.
Lloyds Bank International Ltd.
Malayan Banking Berhad
Manufacturers Hanover Trust Company
Mellon Bank NA
Mercantile Bank Ltd.
Midland Bank Ltd.
Ming Tai Finance Company
Morgan Guaranty Trust Company of New York
Nanyang Commercial Bank Ltd.
National Bank of Pakistan
National Commercial Bank Ltd.
National Westminster Bank Ltd.
North Carolina National Bank
Northern Trust Company
Overseas-Chinese Banking Corporation Ltd.
Overseas Trust Bank Ltd.
Overseas Union Bank Ltd.
Philippine National Bank
Po Sang Bank Ltd.
Rainier International Bank
Republic National Bank of New York
Royal Bank of Canada
Royal Bank of Scotland Ltd.
The Sanwa Bank Ltd.

Shanghai Commercial Bank Ltd.
Sin Hua Trust, Savings and Commercial Bank Ltd.
Societe Generale
State Bank of India
Sumitomo Bank Ltd.
Swiss Bank Corporation
Tai Sang Bank Ltd.
Tai Yau Bank Ltd.
Toronto-Dominion Bank
Underwriters Bank (Overseas) Ltd.
Union Bank of Hong Kong Ltd.
Union Bank of Switzerland
United Chinese Bank Ltd.
United Commercial Bank
United Overseas Bank Ltd.
Wayfoong Finance Ltd.
Westdeutsche Landesbank Girozentrale
Wing Hang Bank Ltd.
Wing Lung Bank Ltd.
Wing On Bank Ltd.
Yien Yeih Commercial Bank Ltd.

Bank Representative Offices:

Allied Bank International
American National Bank & Trust Co. of Chicago
Asia Trust Bank Ltd.
Asian & Pacific Commercial Bank Ltd.
Australia & New Zealand Banking Group Ltd.
Banca Commerciale Italiana
Banca della Svizzera Italiana
Banca Nazionale del Lavoro
Banco Ambrosiano
Banco do Brazil SA

Banco Hispano American
Bangkok Metropolitan Bank
Bank Bumiputra Malaysia Berhad
Bank fur Gemeinwirtschaft AG
Bank Leumi Le-Israel BM
Bank of Bermuda Ltd.
Bank of British Columbia
Bank of Credit and Commerce International
Bank of Credit and Commerce International
  (Overseas) Ltd.
Bank of Hawaii
Bank of Japan
Bank of New South Wales
Bank of Oman Ltd.
Bank of Yokohama
Bank Saderat Iran
Bankers Trust Company
Bankhaus Deak and Company
Banque de l'Union Europeenne
Banque du Rhone et de la Tamise SA
Banque Generale du Luxembourg SA
Banque Vernes et Commerciale de Paris
Bayerische Vereinsbank
BHF Bank
Chase Manhattan Bank (Switzerland)
Cho-Heung Bank Ltd.
Christiania Bank og Kreditkasse
Commercial Bank of Korea Ltd.
Commercial Banking Company of Sydney Ltd.
Commercial Credit International Banking Corporation
Commonwealth Trading Bank of Australia
Continental Illinois National Bank & Trust Co. of Chicago
Copenhagen Handelsbank

Credit Commercial de France
Credit Industriel et Commercial
Credito Italiano
Daiwa Bank Ltd.
Den norske Creditbank
Dow Banking Corporation
Export-Import Bank of Korea
First Bangkok City Bank Ltd.
First Hawaiian Bank
First Interstate Bank of Oregon, NA
First Interstate Bank of Washington, NA
First National Bank in Dallas
GZB-Vienna (Austria) Genossenschaftliche Zentralbank AG
Girard Bank
Gotabanken
Gironzentrale und Bank der osterreichischen Sparkassen AG
Grindlays Bank Ltd.
Habib Bank AG Zurich
Habib Bank Ltd.
Hambros Bank Ltd.
Handelsbank NW
Hokkaido Takushoku Bank Ltd.
Hollandsche Bank-Unie NV
Irving Trust Company
J.P. Morgan (Suisse) SA
Kansallis-Osake-Pankki
Korea Development Bank
Korea First Bank
Kredietbank NV
Kyowa Bank Ltd.
Marine Midland Bank NA
Merrill Lynch International Bank Inc.
Metropolitan Bank and Trust Company

Middle East Bank Ltd.
Midlantic National Bank
Mitsubishi Bank Ltd.
Mitsui Bank Ltd.
National Bank of Australasia Ltd.
National Bank of Canada
National Bank of Detroit
National Bank of New Zealand Ltd.
National Bank of North America
Nederlandsche Middenstandsbank NV
Nippon Credit Bank Ltd.
Nordfinanz-Bank Zurich
Nordia Bank Ltd.
Phibrobank AG
Philadelphia National Bank
Pittsburgh National Bank
Post-och Kreditbanken (PKbanken)
Privatbanken
Producers Bank of the Philippines
Rainier National Bank
Republic National Bank of Dallas NA
Republic National Bank of New York (International) Ltd.
Riggs National Bank
Rothschild Bank AG
The Saitama Bank Ltd.
Scandinavian Bank Ltd.
Seattle-First National Bank
Security Pacific National Bank
Shawmut Bank
Siam Commercial Bank Ltd.
Standard Chartered Bank
State Street Bank and Trust Company
Svenska Handelsbanken

Taiyo Kobe Bank Ltd.
Texas Commerce Bank
Thai Farmers Bank
Thomas Cook Bankers Ltd.
Toyo Trust and Banking Co. Ltd.
Union Bank
Union Planters National Bank of Memphis
Wells Fargo Bank NA
Williams & Glyn's Bank Ltd.
Yasuda Trust & Banking Company Ltd.

Registered deposit-taking companies:

ABN Finance Ltd.
Acme Finance Ltd.
Advance Finance Ltd.
Allied Capital Resources Ltd.
Allied Pacific Corporation
America and Panama Finance Company Ltd.
American Express Finance Ltd.
American United Finance Ltd.
ANZ Finance (Far East) Ltd.
Arab Asian International Ltd.
Argo Enterprises Company Ltd.
Arinfi Asia Ltd.
Asean Merchant Credit and Investment House Ltd.
Asean Nation Internationale Ltd.
Asia Alliance Finance and Investment House Ltd.
Asia Pacific Capital Corporation Ltd.
Asiavest Ltd.
Associated Chinese Finance Company Ltd.
Astro Asia Finance Ltd.
ATB Finance Ltd.
Atlantic Capital Ltd.

Australia-Japan International Finance Ltd.
Ayala Finance (HK) Ltd.
Ayudhya Finance Ltd.
BA Asia Ltd.
BA Finance (Hong Kong) Ltd.
Bahon Finance Ltd.
Bancom International Ltd.
Barclays Asia Ltd.
Barclays Asian Finance Ltd.
Baring Brothers Asia Ltd.
BBL Finance Ltd.
BCCI Finance Ltd.
BCCI Finance International Ltd.
Beacons Finance Ltd.
Belgian Finance Company Ltd.
Beneficial Finance (Hong Kong) Ltd.
Bermuda Finance (Far East) Ltd.
BfG Finance Asia Ltd.
BNP-Daiwa (Hong Kong) Ltd.
BNP Finance (Hong Kong) Ltd.
BNS International (Hong Kong) Ltd.
Bonsun Finance Ltd.
British Columbia Financial Corporation (HK) Ltd.
Broad Rich Finance Company Ltd.
BT Asia Ltd.
BT Finance Ltd.
BUE Asia Ltd.
Bumiputra Malaysia Finance Ltd.
Canadian Eastern Finance Ltd.
Canton Pacific Finance Ltd.
Caranip Finance Company Ltd.
Cash Strong Ltd.
CBC International Finance (Asia) Ltd.

CCIC Finance Ltd.
CCW Finance Company Ltd.
Central Asia Capital Corporation Ltd.
Central Finance Ltd.
Central Leasing (Hong Kong) Ltd.
CF Finance Company Ltd.
Charoen Pokphand Finance Company Ltd.
Chartered Credit (Hong Kong) Ltd.
Chartered Finance (Hong Kong) Ltd.
Chase Manhattan Asia Ltd.
Chau's Brothers Finance Company Ltd.
Che Hsing Finance Company Ltd.
Cheerful Finance Company Ltd.
Chemical Asia Ltd.
Chiao Tung Finance Company Ltd.
Chiao Yue Finance Company Ltd.
Chiap Hua Credit Ltd.
Chiap Luen Finance Ltd.
China Development Finance Company (Hong Kong) Ltd.
China State Finance Company Ltd.
Chiyu Finance Company Ltd.
Chow Sang Sang Finance Ltd.
Chow Tai Fook Finance Ltd.
Chung Nan Finance Company Ltd.
Citicorp Commercial Finance (HK) Ltd.
Citicorp International Ltd.
Commerce International Finance Company (Asia) Ltd.
Commercial Development Finance Ltd.
Cosmos Finance Ltd.
Credit Lyonnais Hongkong (Finance) Ltd.
Credit Suisse Finance Ltd.
Creditland Finance Ltd.
Crocker International (HK) Ltd.

Crown Prince Finance Ltd.
CTB Australia Ltd.
Current Finance Ltd.
Dah Sing Finance Ltd.
Dai-Ichi Kangyo Finance (Hong Kong) Ltd.
Daiwa Overseas Finance Ltd.
Daiwa Securities (HK) Ltd.
DB Finance (Hong Kong) Ltd.
DBS Asia Ltd.
Deak-Perera Finance Ltd.
DG Capital Company Ltd.
Diamond Lease (Hong Kong) Ltd.
Dollar Credit and Financing Ltd.
Dominican Finance Ltd.
Dow Finance Corporation Ltd.
Dubai Oriental Finance Ltd.
East Asia Finance Company Ltd.
Equitable Finance Company (Hong Kong) Ltd.
Estate Finance Ltd.
E. Tung Finance Ltd.
Europa Finance (International) Ltd.
European Asian Finance (HK) Ltd.
Ever Finance Ltd.
Express Finance and Investments Ltd.
Fat Cheung Hing Company Ltd.
Fay Yew Company Ltd.
Filinvest Finance (HK) Ltd.
Financial and Investment Services for Asia Ltd.
First Bangkok City Finance Ltd.
First Canadian Financial Corporation Ltd.
First Chicago Hong Kong Ltd.
First Dallas Asia Ltd.
First Hong Kong Credit Ltd.

First Interstate Asia Ltd.
First Metro International Investment Company Ltd.
First National Boston (Hong Kong) Ltd.
Five Rams Finance Company Ltd.
FNCB Financial Ltd.
Foreign Exchange and Investment Ltd.
Forest Ocean Finance Ltd.
Forex Finance Ltd.
Fuji International Finance (HK) Ltd.
GSP Finance Company Ltd.
GU Finance Ltd.
General Credit Finance and Development Ltd.
Golden Finance Ltd.
Golden Hill Finance Company Ltd.
Great Eagle Finance Company Ltd.
Grindlays Asia Ltd.
Grindlays Finance Ltd.
Gulf Finance Company Ltd.
Habib Finance International Ltd.
Hamburg LB International Ltd.
Hang Lung (Finance) Company Ltd.
Hang Seng Finance Ltd.
Hang Wo Finance and Investments Ltd.
Harbour Finance Company Ltd.
Harvest Finance Company Ltd.
Hawaii Financial Corporation (Hong Kong) Ltd.
HBZ Finance Ltd.
Henderson International Finance Ltd.
HICB Finance Ltd.
Hill Samuel & Company Ltd.
Hind Finance and Industries Ltd.
Hoarestott Finance Ltd.
Hock Finance Holdings Ltd.

Hocomban Finance Ltd.
Hon Hing Finance Company Ltd.
Hondela Finance Ltd.
Hong Fok Finance Company Ltd.
The Hong Kong Chinese International Finance Ltd.
Hong Kong Deposit and Guaranty Company Ltd.
Hong Luen Financial Company Ltd.
Hong Nin Finance Ltd.
Hung Kai Finance Company Ltd.
IBJ Finance Company (Hong Kong) Ltd.
IBU International Finance Ltd.
ICB Finance Ltd.
Imex Finance Ltd.
Impact Finance Ltd.
Inchroy Credit Corporation Ltd.
Indosuez Asia Ltd.
Indosuez Finance Hong Kong Ltd.
Inter-Alpha Asia (Hong Kong) Ltd.
Jardine Fleming (Capital) Ltd.
Jardine Fleming and Company Ltd.
JCG Finance Company Ltd.
J.J. Investment Ltd.
J.P. Morgan (Hong Kong) Ltd.
Ka Wah International Merchant Finance Ltd.
KB Luxembourg (Asia) Ltd.
Kian Nan Financial Ltd.
Kincheng Finance (HK) Ltd.
Kincheng-Tokyo Finance Company Ltd.
King Chong (Finance) Ltd.
King Fook Finance Company Ltd.
King's Finance Company Ltd.
Kingsfield Finance Ltd.
Kingson Finance Ltd.

Kleinwort, Benson Ltd.
Kleinwort, Benson (Hong Kong) Ltd.
KNK Investment International Ltd.
Korea Associated Finance Ltd.
Korea Commercial Finance Ltd.
Korea First Finance Ltd.
K-Rex Finance Ltd.
Kuala Lumpur Finance Company Ltd.
Kuwait Pacific Finance Company Ltd.
Kwong Lee Finance Company Ltd.
Kwong On Finance Ltd.
Kyowa Finance (Hong Kong) Ltd.
LBI Finance (Hong Kong) Ltd.
Legarleon Finance Company Ltd.
Liu Chong Hing Finance Ltd.
LTCB Asia Ltd.
Lu's (Hong Kong) Finance Ltd.
Lung Yuen Finance Company Ltd.
Luxembourg Finance Company Ltd.
Maibl Bermuda (Far East) Ltd.
Malahon Credit and Finance Ltd.
Malayan Finance Company Ltd.
Malaysia American Finance Corporation (HK) Ltd.
Man Sun Finance (International) Corporation Ltd.
Manila CBC Finance (Hong Kong) Ltd.
Manila & Hong Kong Capital Corporation Ltd.
Manufacturers Hanover Asia Ltd.
Manufacturers' Mutual Finance Ltd.
Marac Hong Kong Ltd.
Merban Asia Ltd.
Merchant Guaranty Ltd.
Metropolitan Finance Corporation Ltd.
Middle East Finance International Ltd.

Midland Finance (HK) Ltd.
Mitsubishi International Finance Ltd.
Mitsui Finance Asia Ltd.
Mitsui Trust Finance (Hong Kong) Ltd.
Multi-Credit Finance Company Ltd.
Multilight Credit Ltd.
Multinational Securities and Investment Company Ltd.
Nanyang Finance Company Ltd.
NATCAN Finance (Asia) Ltd.
National Westminster (Hong Kong) Ltd.
NCNB (Asia) Ltd.
Neways Finance Ltd.
Nippon Credit International (Hong Kong) Ltd.
Nomura International (Hong Kong) Ltd.
Nordic Asia Ltd.
OCBC Finance (Hong Kong) Ltd.
Oman International Finance Ltd.
Ong Finance (HK) Ltd.
Ontario Finance and Investment Company Ltd.
Orient Leasing (Asia) Ltd.
Orion Pacific Ltd.
OTB Finance Ltd.
OUB Finance (HK) Ltd.
Overseas Express Finance Corporation Ltd.
Overseas Union Finance Ltd.
Pan Seas Finance & Investment Ltd.
Panin International Finance Corporation Ltd.
Paribas Asia Ltd.
PCI Capital (Hong Kong) Ltd.
Philadelphia International Finance Co.—Hong Kong Ltd.
Philippine Finance and Investment Company Ltd.
Philmont Finance and Investment Company Ltd.
Philtrust Finance Ltd.

Pierson, Heldring & Pierson NV
PNB International Finance Ltd.
Po Fung Finance Company Ltd.
Producers Finance and Investment Ltd.
Public Finance (HK) Ltd.
Rainier International Finance Company Ltd.
Rama Credit Ltd.
Renown Credit Ltd.
RNB Finance (Hong Kong) Ltd.
Robina Credit Ltd.
N.M. Rothschild & Sons (Hong Kong) Ltd.
Royal Scot Finance Company Ltd.
RoyEast Investments Ltd.
Sai Shing Investment and Finance Ltd.
Saitama International (Hong Kong) Ltd.
Sanwa International Finance Ltd.
SBC Finance (Asia) Ltd.
SB India Hong Kong Finance Ltd.
Scandinavian Far East Ltd.
Schroders and Chartered Ltd.
Search Asia Ltd.
Seattle-First Asia Ltd.
Security Pacific Credit (Hong Kong) Ltd.
Shacom Finance Ltd.
Sharikat Safety Finance Company (Hong Kong) Ltd.
Shearson Finance (Asia) Ltd.
Shun Sing Finance Company Ltd.
Siam Commercial Finance Ltd.
Sin Hua Finance Company Ltd.
Sing-Ho Finance Company Ltd.
Sino-Thai Finance Ltd.
Siu On Finance Company Ltd.
Societe Generale Finance (Hong Kong) Ltd.

Solid Pacific Finance Ltd.
Southeast Asia Properties and Finance (Credit) Ltd.
State Investment House (Hong Kong) Ltd.
Stephens Finance Ltd.
Stephil Finance Ltd.
Sumitomo Finance (Asia) Ltd.
Sumitomo Trust Finance (HK) Ltd.
Summa International Finance Company (HK) Ltd.
Sun Hung Kai Finance Company Ltd.
Sun Light Finance Company Ltd.
Sun Poh Shing Finance Company Ltd.
Supreme Finance Ltd.
Sward Finance Ltd.
Tai Sang Finance Ltd.
Tai Shing Finance Company Ltd.
Taiyo Kobe Finance Hongkong Ltd.
Takugin International (Asia) Ltd.
Tat Lee Finance Singapore Ltd.
Tesoro Finance and Investment Company Ltd.
Tetra Finance (HK) Ltd.
Thai Farmers Finance and Investment Ltd.
Thai Mercantile Development Finance Ltd.
Thai-Overseas Investment and Finance Company Ltd.
Thai United Finance Company Ltd.
Thye Hong Commercial and Finance Company Ltd.
Times Finance Ltd.
TKM (Far East) Ltd.
Tokai Asia Ltd.
Tokyo Finance (Asia) Ltd.
Tokyo Leasing (Hongkong) Ltd.
Toronto-Dominion (Hong Kong) Ltd.
Toyo Trust Asia Ltd.
Trade Development Finance (Asia) Ltd.

Uban-Arab Japanese Finance Ltd.
Union Finance Ltd.
Unipacific Finance (Internationale) Ltd.
Unistock Finance Ltd.
United Chinese Finance Company Ltd.
United Merchants Finance Ltd.
UT Finance Ltd.
Vernes Asia Ltd.
Vietnam Finance Company Ltd.
Wales Australia Ltd.
Wa Pei Finance Company Ltd.
Wardley Ltd.
Washington International Ltd.
Wayfoong Credit Ltd.
Wells Fargo Asia Ltd.
WestLB Asia Ltd.
Whitehall Finance Ltd.
Widely Credits Ltd.
Wing Hang Finance Company Ltd.
Wing Hong Finance and Management Ltd.
Wing Lung Finance Ltd.
Wing On Finance Company Ltd.
Wisdom Finance Company Ltd.
WOC Finance Company Ltd.
Worms Asia Ltd.
Yasuda Trust and Finance (Hong Kong) Ltd.
Yick Yuen Finance and Development Ltd.
Yien Yieh Finance Company Ltd.
Yokohama Asia Ltd.

MONTSERRAT

American Bank of Commerce Ltd.
American Overseas Bank Ltd.

Century Overseas Bank Ltd.
Chase Overseas Bank Ltd.
City International Bank Ltd.
Colonial Overseas Bank Ltd.
Continental Overseas Bank Ltd.
European Overseas Bank Ltd.
Fidelity International Bank Ltd.
First Security International Bank Ltd.
Foreign Commerce Bank Ltd.
Gibraltar International Bank Ltd.
Handelsbank von Montserrat Ltd.
International Overseas Bank Ltd.
Investors International Bank Ltd.
J. David Banking Company Ltd.
LaSalle Overseas Bank Ltd.
Manhattan International Bank Ltd.
Manufacturers Overseas Bank Ltd.
Merchants International Bank Ltd.
Metropolitan Overseas Bank Ltd.
Morgan Overseas Bank Ltd.
North American Overseas Bank Ltd.
Republic International Bank Ltd.
Security Overseas Bank Ltd.
Sterling Overseas Bank Ltd.
Surety International Bank Ltd.
Swiss International Bank Ltd.
Swiss Overseas Bank Ltd.
Union Chartered Bank Ltd.
Union International Bank Ltd.
United Bank of Commerce Ltd.
United International Bank Ltd.
W.C.T. Bank Ltd.

NETHERLANDS ANTILLES

Algemene Bank Nederland NV
Allied Bank International NV
Antilliaanse Bank Unie NV
Antilliaanse Financierings Maatschappij 'Anfimij' NV
Amro Bank Overseas NV
Banco Popular Antillano
Bank of America
Bank of Nova Scotia
Caribbean Mercantile Bank NV
Citibank NA
Citicorp Overseas Finance Corporation NV
Chase Manhattan
Curacao Tokyo Holding
Curacaoosche Hypotheekbank NV
Drexel Burnham International Bank Ltd. NV
F van Lanschot Bankiers (Curacao) NV
First Curacao International Bank NV
Inarco International Bank NV
Interunion Antilles NV
Maduro & Curiel's Bank
Nederlandsche Handel-Maatschappij, Trustkantoor
  Curacao, Trustmaatschappij van de A.B.N.
  (Curacao) NV
NV Spaar en Beleenbank van Curacao
Partnership Pacific Bank NV
Pierson Heldring & Pierson (Curacao) NV
Trustmaatschappij van de Algemene Bank Nederland
  (St. Maarten) NV
Windward Islands Bank

PANAMA

Official Banks:

Banco Nacional de Panama
Caja de Ahorros

Private Banks:

Algemene Bank Nederland NV
Banco Agro-Industrial y Comercial de Panama SA
Banco de Bogota SA
Banco do Brasil SA
Banco Cafetero SA
Banco de Colombia SA
Banco Comercial Antioqueno SA
Banco Comercial de Panama SA
Banco Comercial Transatlantico SA
Banco del Comercio SA
Banco Consolidado (Panama) SA
Banco de Credito Internacional SA
Banco do Estado de Sao Paulo SA
Banco Exterior SA
Banco Fiduciario de Panama SA
Banco Ganadero SA
Banco General SA
Banco de Iberoamerica SA
Banco Industrial Colombiano de Panama SA
Banco Internacional de Costa Rica SA
Banco Internacional de Panama SA
Banco Interoceanico de Panama SA
Banco Latinoamericana de Exportaciones SA (Bladex)
Banco Panameno de la Vivienda SA
Banco Real SA

Banco de Santander y Panama SA
Banco Sudamericano de Desarrollo
Banco Sudameris Internacional SA
Banco de Ultramar SA
Banco Union CA de Venezuela
Bank of Credit and Commerce International (Overseas) Ltd.
Bank of London and South America Ltd.
Bank of Nova Scotia
Bank of Tokyo Ltd.
Bankers Trust Company
Banque Anval SA
Chase Manhattan Bank NA
Citibank NA
Dai-Ichi Kangyo Bank
Deutsch Sudamerikanische Bank AG
First National Bank of Boston
First National Bank of Chicago
International Commercial Bank of China
Korea Exchange Bank
Lloyds Bank International (Bahamas) Ltd.
Marine Midland Bank
Merrill Lynch International Bank Inc.
Mitsui Bank Ltd.
Primer Banco de Ahorros
Republic National Bank Inc.
Sanwa Bank Ltd.
Sociedad de Banca Suiza (Panama)
State Bank of India
Sumitomo Bank Ltd.
Tower International Bank Inc.
Trade Development Bank (Overseas)

International License:

Adela International Financing Company
American Express International Banking Corporation
BAII (Middle East) Inc.
Banco Aleman Panameno SA
Banco Andino
Banco del Centro
Banco Colombo Americano SA
Banco Euroamericano SA
Banco Mercantil y Agricola SA
El Banco Metropolitano SA
Banco de la Nacion Argentina
Banco Del Pacifico (Panama)
Banco Popular del Ecuador
Banco Promotor del Comercio
Banco Provincial SAICA
Banco Rio de la Plata (Panama) SA
Banco Rio de la Plata SA
Banco Santa Cruz de la Sierra (Panama) SA
Bank of Commerce and Finance SA
Bank of Investment and Trade Inc.
Bank of Tokyo (Panama) SA
Banque Nationale de Paris
Banque de Paris et des Pays-Bas
Banque Sudameris
Citicorp International Group SA
Credit Commercial de France (Panama) SA
Credit Lyonnais
Dibeag Banking Corporation
Discount Bank Overseas
Discount Bank (Overseas) Ltd.
First Interamerican Bank SA
Interamerican Bank Corporation SA

International Union Bank SA
Libra International Bank SA
Republic National Bank of New York (Panama) SA
Security Pacific Bank (Panama) SA
Societe Generale
Swiss Bank Corporation (Overseas)
Toronto-Dominion Bank Panama SA
Towerbank Overseas Inc.
Western Intercontinental Bank Corporation
Weston Banking Corporation

Representation License:

Banco Espagnol de Credito
Banco Nacional de Cuba
Banco Regional Sur Medio y Callao
Banco Leumi Le Israel BM
Daiwa Bank Ltd.
Dresdner Bank AG
Ibero America Bank Aktiengesellschaft
Philadelphia National Bank
Sanwa Bank Ltd.
Security Pacific National Bank
Toronto-Dominion Bank

MARIANA ISLANDS

American Bank and Trust Company Ltd.
American Chartered Bank Ltd.
American Commerce Bank Ltd.
American Savings Bank
Asia Pacific Development Bank Ltd.
Asian Credit Bank Ltd.

Asian Commerce Bank Ltd.
Bank of Guam
Bank of Hawaii
Bank of Saipan
California First Bank
Colonial Bank of Commerce Ltd.
Colonial Chartered Bank Ltd.
Commercial Bank of Commerce Ltd.
Commercial Chartered Bank Ltd.
Commercial Credit Bank Ltd.
Continental Bank & Trust Company Ltd.
Continental Bank of Commerce Ltd.
Continental Chartered Bank Ltd.
Dominion Bank of Commerce Ltd.
Dominion Chartered Bank Ltd.
Dominion Commerce Bank Ltd.
European Bank of Commerce Ltd.
European Credit Bank Ltd.
Fidelity Bank of Commerce Ltd.
Fidelity Chartered Bank Ltd.
First American Bank Ltd.
First Fidelity Bank Ltd.
First Global Bank Ltd.
First International Bank Ltd.
First North Western Bank Ltd.
First Pacific Bank Ltd.
First Republic Bank Ltd.
Gibraltar Bank of Commerce Ltd.
Gibraltar Chartered Bank Ltd.
Global Bank and Trust Company Ltd.
Global Bank of Commerce Ltd.
Global Credit Bank Ltd.
Heritage Bank and Trust Company Ltd.

Heritage Chartered Bank Ltd.
Merchants Bank of Commerce Ltd.
Merchants Chartered Bank Ltd.
Merchants Credit Bank Ltd.
North American Bank and Trust Company Ltd.
North American Chartered Bank Ltd.
North Western Bank of Commerce Ltd.
North Western Chartered Bank Ltd.
Pacific Bank and Trust Company Ltd.
Pacific Bank of Commerce Ltd.
Republic Bank and Trust Company Ltd.
Republic Bank of Commerce Ltd.
Royal Chartered Bank Ltd.
Royal Credit Bank Ltd.

TURKS AND CAICOS

Barclays Bank International Ltd.
Chartered Trust Company Ltd.
European American Bank & Trust Ltd.
Exchange National Bank Ltd.
First Caribbean Trust Company Ltd.
First National City Bank & Trust Company Ltd.
International Bank for Investment & Commerce
Oxford International Bank & Trust Company Ltd.

VANUATU

American Finance Group Ltd.
Ample Asian Bank and Trust Company Ltd.
Armour General Bank Ltd.
Asia Credit International Bank Ltd.

Asiac Bank Ltd.
Asian and Pacific Commercial Bank Ltd.
Asian Bank Ltd.
Australia and New Zealand Banking Group Ltd.
Australia and New Zealand Savings Bank Ltd.
Australian International Bank Ltd.
Ayala International Capital Ltd.
Ayala International Finance (Vila) Ltd.
Bank of New South Wales
Bank Gutzwiller, Kurz, Bungener (Overseas) Ltd.
Bank of New South Wales Savings Bank Ltd.
Bank of South Asia Ltd.
Banque de Montpierre Ltd.
Banque Nationale de Paris
Banque Nationale de Paris (Vila) Ltd.
Barclays Bank International Ltd.
BBL International Bank Ltd.
BIL (Vila) Bank Ltd.
Binning Pacific Bank Ltd.
Chithead International Bank Ltd.
Commercial Bank of Australia Ltd.
Commercial Bank of Hong Kong Overseas Ltd.
Crorcoridge Ltd.
Davidson Bank Ltd.
Dominion Banking Ltd.
Equities Bank Ltd.
European Bank Ltd.
Fidelity Bank of Commerce Ltd.
First Chicago Bank Ltd.
First Europe Bank Ltd.
GCG Bank Ltd.
Global Bank Ltd.
Golden Peninsula Bank Ltd.

GPF International Bank Ltd.
Grand Credit Bank Ltd.
Hong Kong and Shanghai Banking Corporation
Inter-Alpha Asia (Pacific) Ltd.
International Bank of Washington (Far East) Ltd.
Investors Trust Ltd.
Jibsen Capital Bank Ltd.
Kredietbank Luxembourg (Pacific) Ltd.
Marine and Merchant Bank Ltd.
McKenney Bank Ltd.
Mercantile Bank Ltd.
Meridian Financial Ltd.
Melanesia International Trust Company Ltd.
Multilight Bank International Ltd.
Multinational Bank (Vanuatu) Ltd.
National Bank of Canada (Pacific) Ltd.
Pacific Bank Ltd.
Pacific Credit Bank Ltd.
Pacific Investment Bank Ltd.
Putney International Bank Ltd.
Security and General Bank Ltd.
SHK Bank Ltd.
SIH (Vila) Ltd.
South East Asia Bank Ltd.
South Pacific Bank Ltd.
Stanbridge International Bank Ltd.
State Investment House (Hong Kong) Ltd.
Summa International Bank Ltd.
Trans-Pacific International Bank Ltd.
Trident (Vila) Ltd.
Union Credit Bank Ltd.
Unipacific Bank Ltd.
Universal Bank Ltd.

Wardley Investments (N.H.) Ltd.
Wardley Ltd.
Wardley (Vila) Ltd.
Western Pacific Bank Ltd.
Westham Bank Ltd.
Worldwide Guaranty Bank Ltd.
Ying Pak International Bank Ltd.
Youker International Bank Ltd.

APPENDIX B

Transcript of the Best Lectures at the International Conference on Offshore Banking

The first major conference ever presented for investors and businessmen on offshore banking was held April 5 and 6, 1982, at the Los Angeles Century Plaza Hotel. The International Conference on Offshore Banking was sponsored and presented by WFI Corp.

The world's most knowledgeable experts spoke on every aspect of offshore banking. All the speakers underscored one theme in particular—offshore banking can help virtually every investor or businessman overcome the ills of the American economy. As one attendee remarked, "Offshore banking is a tool that makes it possible for me to use the techniques, knowledge and resources available outside the U.S., to make money, avoid the IRS and keep my financial and business affairs private."

One speaker in particular seemed to impress everyone. He spoke about why the American economy is in such bad shape and what investors or businessmen can do to stay ahead. Dr. Bradford Cornell, Ph.D. and associate professor of finance and economics at UCLA, captioned his lecture, "Are You Waiting for a Solution to the Problems of the U.S. Economy." Here is a synopsis of what Dr. Cornell said:

"Before discussing why offshore banking is important to you, I would like to give you an overview of the current U.S. economy and outline where the major problems are. Certainly one of the major problems is government deficits. The U.S. deficit for the upcoming fiscal year will be about $120 billion, and that is due to high interest rates, the continued recession, reduced tax collection, and the continuing unemployment and the concomitant payment of unemployment benefits. Knowing that accountants do funny things with numbers, you might think that the $120 billion debt is not as bad as it sounds, but actually it is substantially worse when you examine it.

"The $120 billion I have mentioned is the deficit of the U.S. Treasury, and not all government borrowing goes through the Treasury. There are many other government agencies, like the Home Loan Bank, that borrow money independent of the Treasury, and the combined deficit of these agencies in recent years has been running about one-third that of the U.S. Treasury—or about $30 billion in the upcoming year. Moreover, besides these U.S. government agencies, there are all the state and local governments that will be borrowing money as well.

"Underneath this situation is the even more serious problem of the Social Security system. The current value of Social Security's obligations exceeds the current value of the projected tax receipts by $1.25 trillion or more. So barring major reform in Social Security, and barring budget cuts and tax increases, it appears that the Federal Government will be into the capital markets in increasing amounts in the years to come.

"Now, I would not care very much about the federal government being in the capital market for a few hundred million if it were not for the fact that the government is competing with me for those funds it's borrowing. As the government competes for those funds, it bids up the interest rate. What can happen in this case has been called 'crowding out' or 'pricing out.' The government enters the market, bids for funds and pushes up the real interest to a point where money becomes prohibitively expensive for many private borrowers—that is, they are crowded out of the market.

"Many people claim that if the Federal Reserve would loosen up and let the money supply grow faster, we would not have this current problem. But I do not believe it is a fair criticism, for the money supply during the last five years has been growing at about 5 percent per year. This growth rate is well above what we had in 1955, yet interest rates in real terms as well as dollar terms are much higher than that. In fact, the pressure on the Federal Reserve is an indication that the government's finances are out of control. For it is the Federal Reserve that offers the government one way not to push borrowers out of the market. Specifically, it can monetize the government's debt simply by printing new money and buying the debt. But then, instead of pushing borrowers out of the market, what we have is inflation.

"Clearly one problem we face today is the government budget and whether we can get it under control. If not, are we going to have continuing inflation, or will real interest rates be pushed up to a point where so many private borrowers are pushed out of the market that we have an even deeper recession?

"Another serious problem with the U.S. economy is referred to as the 'productivity crisis' for American industry. Productivity, most simply, is how much you can produce in an hour or day, and the key to productivity is the tools you work with. After World War II, U.S. workers had much better tools than Japanese and German workers; therefore; they produced more and commanded higher wages. But in the ensuing years, Japanese and German workers have invested substantially more of their earnings than have American workers, and that investment has ultimately led to new plants and better tools. Today, the productivity of Japanese and German workers is close to or even higher than that of American workers, but nonetheless American workers are still paid substantially higher wages. This means American business may be paying up to twice as much for labor that is no longer twice as productive. Consequently, some American products, like automobiles, are not competitive in the marketplace.

"One solution to this crisis is simply to close our doors to foreign products. But this hurts the American consumer by denying access to high quality, inexpensive products. Moreover, closing our doors to trade would cause other countries to retaliate by closing their doors to American products. If we therefore decide we do not want that solution and instead want to keep our doors open to foreign trade, then the U.S. will have to fall relative to the Japanese. Furthermore, U.S. productivity and savings will have to rise in order for our products to remain competitive.

"In view of these problems with the U.S. economy, clearly we need some new program out of Washington. But we need to realize that any economic improvement takes place over the long haul. The Japanese were able to bring their country from the ravages of war to their current success not overnight but through 30 years of government taxes and policies that allowed them to save and develop. It will take us a long time as well.

"Now, considering these problems from the perspective of the investor, my point is that we should not wait for economic recovery in the U.S. Let me illustrate what the investor should do by an example. Suppose I offer you a bet of 2-to-1 odds on the flip of a coin, heads I win and tails you win. The catch is that we bet a million dollars, so you pay me a million if you lose. Probably most of you would not take that bet simply because you are smart enough not to put all your eggs in one basket. A better way to protect yourself would be to diversify by making many small bets, so that if a few bets did not pay off, others would.

"The same principle applies if you concentrate your investments in the U.S. and rely on the improvement of the U.S. economy; in a very real sense, you are putting all your eggs in one basket. It would be better to diversify by putting some of your wealth in the U.S. and some in Singapore, Hong Kong, etc.

"As an example, consider that the New York Stock Exchange appreciated by 120.4 percent from 1970 to 1981. It sounds good, except that the U.S. price level doubled during the same period. So in real terms, you had 20 percent more money, but that 20 percent more would only buy 60 cents' worth of goods in 1981. Thus, your turnover in that ten-year period would have been a minus 40 percent. On the other hand, the Hong Kong stock market over that same ten-year period appreciated 742.3 percent, the Singapore stock market appreciated 423 percent, Japan 170 percent and Canada 135 percent, and that is just stock markets. There may have been other overseas investments, for example in real estate, that might have done better.

"My point is that when you buy stocks, you do not go with only a single company, so there is no reason for you to hold your investments to just one country. Diversification, as always, is a good rule."

The conference featured other speakers from around the world—including the well-known Mark Skousen. The information presented, in many cases, was revealed for the first time. I have edited the actual transcripts of all the lectures, kept the essentials, and now present you with a digest of the best speeches presented at the 1982 International Conference on Offshore Banking.

Background and Growth of Offshore Banking
by Robert Buchsbaum

For the 137 years following the birth of our nation in 1776, there was no permanent income tax in the United States. In fact, in 1895 the United States Supreme Court held that a direct tax on income was unconstitutional. But then in 1913, with the passing of the Sixteenth Amendment, the Congress unfortunately did enact a tax on income.

The legal avoidance of that tax on income is one of the three main reasons for offshore banking. Reason number two is the freedom to conduct business without burdensome regulations. Reason number three is the ability to conduct financial transactions in total and complete financial privacy. The growth of offshore banking and the attendant growth of the tax-related industry are the result of these three fundamental desires of any businessman.

More precisely, in terms of historical development, offshore banking began as the U.S. and other governments proposed higher and higher taxes and as the governmental bureaucracies imposed increasingly burdensome regulations. In response, the business community sought new alternatives. One alternative was offered by some of the smaller and less developed countries that wanted to attract business and capital. Specifically, these countries passed business-related legislation providing for the three key points of legal tax avoidance, freedom from burdensome business regulations, and financial privacy.

The incentives for these less developed countries are based on simple economics. For example, the host government usually charges an annual license fee which, in effect, is an annuity to that country. In many cases, especially in less developed countries, that annuity is the equivalent of an average salary. Thus, each new banking license is the equivalent of a new job.

Another incentive derives from the common requirement that some sort of cash account or cash reserve be maintained in the host country. The benefit is that the host country thereby develops new working capital without any cost. Moreover, there is great potential for more diversified growth. For as more and more business is conducted through the host country, tourism and capital investment generally tend to follow.

Countries that offer the benefits of no taxes, financial privacy, and no burdensome regulations are tax havens. But there are differences that must be taken into consideration.

One point to consider is that as offshore banking has grown and matured, it has become apparent that there are two different philosophies among countries concerning their rate of growth. Some host countries are interested in getting as much business as possible as soon as possible. As a result, they tend not to scrutinize business people too well. The alternative philosophy is more concerned with long-term, controlled growth. Countries with this philosophy may exclude certain business people they regard as *personae non grata.* Thereby, it is believed that in the long run the country will develop a better reputation and its financial development will be more long lasting. So in selecting a tax haven, that is one thing that must be considered—the reputation of the country.

A second point is that there are different kinds of tax havens. Some are better for ship registration, some better for insurance companies, some for trust companies, some for real estate companies, some for offshore banking and some for onshore banking. Thus, many different factors unique to your particular situation must be considered in the selection of a tax haven. The purpose of this international conference is to provide you with enough information to make that selection.

Background and Growth of Offshore Banking

by Dr. Bradford Cornell

Most people think of "money" as dollar bills. But when banks think about money, what they really think about are computer entries—that is, large records that say who owns what right to what wealth. Significantly, these computer entries can be moved to an offshore bank very quickly and essentially cost-free. This helps explain why and how major banks have moved offshore.

To understand how this works, let us suppose that I want to make an offshore deposit—to a bank in London, for example—through my bank in Los Angeles. First, I need a large enough deposit, and that usually means $100,000 or more. Next, I will be quoted an interest rate by the bank. If I accept that rate, I will be credited with a bank deposit.

Now, does my bank in Los Angeles then take one hundred thousand dollar bills and fly them to London? Absolutely not. Instead, the computer in my bank simply credits my deposit in a bank memory called "London" instead of a bank of memory called "United States." For legal purposes, my money is in London and I have what is called a Eurodollar deposit. But in fact, all that happened was a simple, costless electronic transfer for the bank.

If this is all there is to it, then why have so many major banks moved offshore? From the banker's point of view, the most important reason is that there are no reserve requirements in offshore banking. On any domestic deposit in the U.S., a bank is required to hold reserved deposits with the Federal Reserve System, and the Fed pays no interest whatsoever on those deposits. Thus, a bank has to take some of your money and put it with the Fed and earn no interest on it. And to the extent that the bank has to pay that cost, you can be sure they are going to pass the cost on to you. As you and the bank will earn less because of this, that is one incentive you both have for making financial transactions, not through New York but through London or Singapore or the Cayman Islands.

Another incentive is that once your deposit is credited in the computer bank as being in London or Singapore, it is under the rule of foreign authorities, not the U.S. Federal Reserve System. That means there are absolutely no interest rate regulations on what the bank can pay you. It can pay a completely competitive market rate of interest.

Moreover, the bank has no lending restrictions offshore. So it can lend your deposit out to a borrower who is willing to pay the highest rate of interest. That again makes it possible for the bank to pay you a greater rate of interest than it could in the U.S.

As you would expect, these factors have allowed banks to make money by moving offshore. The reason being, that without the reserve requirements or the lending and interest rate regulations, banks can do business more competitively and profitably, passing out part of the benefit to you as a borrower or a depositor.

To provide you with another explanation of how this works, let me stress the basic principle with a specific example. Suppose there is a retail company in Los Angeles with approximately 60 million in bank debt. They are dealing with a major bank, also headquartered in Los Angeles, and they are discussing their borrowing rate. It so happens that if the company is willing to borrow offshore, the bank can offer them not just the U.S. prime rate but also one-half over what is called LIBOR, which is the London Interbank Rate. LIBOR is usually a point or two below the prime rate. So in this case, a Los Angeles-based company can borrow from a Los Angeles-based bank at about one-half to one percent below the U.S. prime rate. The transaction supposedly is taking place in London, but that is just because the computer says so, since that is where everything is credited and where the deposit is. But as far as the borrower is concerned, his bank and banker are in Los Angeles and he is paying the rate below prime.

Let me reemphasize here the important point that it is possible for a bank in Los Angeles to deal with a depositer and a borrower both in Los Angeles and to run the operation through a bank in London or Singapore. This is simply because the deposit will be credited offshore in the computer bank and the loan will come from there too.

Now, continuing with the example. What about the company that makes a London deposit? Would not they be getting a lower rate on their money? The answer is no, since they are getting a higher rate than if they bought a domestic CB—about a half point higher with a London deposit. So in this case, the depositor gets a better rate and the borrower gets a lower rate by virtue of offshore banking.

And the bank does not lose either. By not having a lot of reserve requirements and regulatory overhead, the bank profits too.

As evidence of this profitability, consider that the Bank of America in 1970 earned 19 percent of its total income offshore, and by 1980 the figure was up to 50 percent. Similarly, by

1980, Citibank was earning almost 75 percent of its money offshore. That does not mean that 75 percent of their bankers were overseas; it means that the actual intermediation took place offshore.

Since the offshore banking business is so profitable and less regulated, it is to be expected that there would be tremendous growth in the amount of offshore intermediation. In fact, it has been perhaps the greatest growth industry in the world in recent years. Specifically, in 1965 the total offshore market in terms of all deposits was about $24 billion. By the end of 1981, the market was approximately $1,500 billion, or $1.5 trillion. That is a growth of almost 100 times in sixteen years.

Given the tremendous incentive for the banks to move offshore and the explosive growth in deposits, the next question is "Who is involved in this business?" For an answer, think of any major corporation you are dealing with, from the local drug-trade chain like Thrifty in Los Angeles to the big companies like IBM and General Motors. Virtually every major corporation you can think of is involved in the offshore banking business. By the same token, virtually every major bank from every country in the world is involved in the offshore market.

To summarize, what the offshore market has offered is a more competitive, less regulated and freer way of doing business. In response to this, all the major banks and major corporations have become aggressively involved.

Powers and Benefits of Offshore Banking— For Individuals
by Adrian Day

Just before the outbreak of World War II, a prosperous Jewish-German businessman named Lance Lubeck was forced to flee his country so quickly that he arrived in the United States with no money in his pockets. Luckily, over the years Lubeck had smuggled 20,000 German marks into a Swiss bank without the knowledge of German authorities. By getting that money into the U.S., Lubeck was able to start life anew. The point of the story is that without offshore banking, Mr. Lubeck would not have been able to get his money and he would have been a penniless immigrant.

Cases similar to Lubeck's have been occurring for the last thirty years and continue to happen all the time. Think of the Vietnamese fleeing Vietnam, and the people who fled Chile and Nicaragua. Such cases represent the main reason for using an offshore bank—that is, for insurance against the ultimate financial disaster to yourself. We pray that we will never need this kind of insurance, but it is only prudent to have a certain amount of our assets outside the country in case of catastrophes.

Apart from this ultimate insurance purpose, there are many other reasons why an investor should use an offshore bank. Another reason is for protection against a personal financial disaster, such as a ruinous divorce settlement or a malpractice suit. If we have assets abroad, we can structure ourselves so these assets are not vulnerable to attack here in the U.S.

A third reason is that of tax avoidance. Quite simply, an offshore bank becomes a place for worldwide investments which, if not reported, would not be subject to U.S. income taxes. By the same token, we can build up our capital out of the country so that when we die, 50, 60 or whatever percent of our hard earned assets will not be given to Uncle Sam. Instead, we can pass on a few more of our assets to our heirs.

I should point out that a U.S. citizen, of course, has the obligation to report and pay tax on income received anywhere in the world; and tax on offshore profits is exactly the same as tax on domestic income. But my point is that it is possible to use an offshore bank in a secret jurisdiction so as to avoid paying taxes on income.

It is obvious that the three reasons mentioned so far depend on secrecy and, to a major degree, on illegality. There are, however, many other reasons for offshore banking that do not depend on illegality in the slightest. The first of these reasons is that of greater banking services. America lags far behind most of the rest of the world in services offered by banks. For example, NOW accounts have been in the U.S. for only a few years, but many banks around the world have had them for decades. Another example is foreign currency checking accounts, which are quite normal in most offshore banks. A third service is multicurrency checking accounts, where you have an account denominated in one currency, such as U.S. dollars, but you can write checks on that account in any currency you like. These are just a few of the many points that illustrate that offshore banks have a far greater range of services than U.S. banks.

A second legal reason for using offshore banks is confidentiality. This can be apart from secrecy and illegality. For you might want to report all your transactions and obey all U.S. rules and regulations, but at the same time you might not want a lot of other people to have access to information in your account—people such as other government agencies, creditors and perhaps even your wife.

A third nonillegal reason is the greater range of investment opportunities available to someone with assets outside the country. In particular, I am referring to investments that are regulated in the U.S. and that U.S. citizens consequently cannot freely purchase. An example would be foreign-based mutual funds. Mutual funds have to be registered with the Securities and Exchange Commission (SEC) in order for the offering company to solicit business in the U.S. Many companies decline registering with the SEC because of the burdensome paperwork and regulations; but that does not mean anything is wrong with these mutual funds. A U.S. citizen is allowed to purchase into such a mutual fund, but he has to go about it on his own and he has to be the one to initiate the action. Moreover, there are some mutual funds that want to avoid all hassles with the SEC and simply will not accept investments from U.S. citizens. In such a case, a U.S. citizen wishing to invest in the mutual fund would have to operate through an offshore entity. An example of another type of investment would be gold-backed annuities, which are illegal in the U.S. but available in Britain and other countries. If you are interested in a gold-backed annuity, you would have to obtain it through an offshore entity, such as an offshore bank.

A fourth legal reason for offshore banking is safety. This may surprise those who think of offshore banks as small, shaky institutions in the Caribbean Islands. There are a few of those, but I think the record of the last twenty years bears out that the vast majority of offshore banks have been quite safe and reputable institutions. It is true that most banks abroad are not government-insured, so it is incumbent upon the investor to look at the offshore bank's financial statement, especially if we are putting in substantial funds. I would say that for most normal investment situations, we should probably restrict our banking to long established banks. In particular, I like using banks of second or third jurisdictions—for example, Canadian banks in the Bahamas or Swiss banks in London that are highly reputable and whose names we all know. I mind using the banks in the home country because they are always subject to more regulation than they are in the third country.

Powers and Benefits of Offshore Banking— For Corporations

by Dr. Alan Shapiro

The advantages of offshore banking relate largely to the reasons for the existence of offshore banking. Basically, it involves arbitrating in the areas of tax management and regulatory management.

There are significantly lower regulatory costs to offshore banking, the reasons of which are listed below.

(1) Offshore banks are not required to maintain reserves against depository liabilities.

(2) There are no FDIC fees.

(3) Offshore banks manage to avoid a wide range of minor but costly regulatory constraints that are faced by domestic banks.

(4) Offshore banks are not required to allocate credit to certain borrowers at below-market rates.

(5) Offshore banks are not forced to purchase certain types of securities such as government debt; they are free to allocate their resources as they choose.

(6) There are no credit ceilings that restrict offshore banks from going after profitable business.

(7) There are no official limits on deposit rate, such as Regulation Q that exists in the United States, nor are there ceilings on lending rates.

This ability to reduce regulatory costs means that offshore banks can provide higher interest rates on deposits while simultaneously demanding lower rates on loans.

Offshore banks also have the ability to avoid taxes by selecting low-tax or no-tax jurisdictions. Avoidance of taxes again allows offshore banks to provide higher interest rates on deposits and lower interest rates on loans than can U.S. banks.

Offshore banking also permits greater efficiency. This is due to the absence of any regulations on entry and expansion. In effect, there is significantly greater competition in offshore banking than purely domestic banking, and this competition fosters greater efficiency.

One additional point is that offshore banking generally permits fewer political risks. There is a reduced risk of government regulations since these offshore banks have great mobility. They can, in effect, pick themselves up and move to another location, and governments recognize that. Offshore banks also permit individuals and corporations in politically risky countries to transfer their funds to these institutions and, therefore, there is less danger of home-country expropriation or control of funds.

When I am talking about offshore banking, I am primarily referring to the Euromarkets, the markets for taking in deposits and lending out these deposits in a currency. The Euromarkets, or "Eurodollar" markets, basically involve the markets overseas for deposits of dollars in other currencies outside their home countries. The specific advantages to borrowers of offshore banking, in this regard, are as follows:

(1) The offshore banks can provide the lower tax and regulatory costs that enable them to lend out money at lower costs.

(2) Competition forces offshore banks to lend out money at lower costs.

Initially, borrowers were major firms. But now, even domestic firms, virtually unknown, are learning to rely on Eurocurrency loans. Primarily, when local credit is tight and interest rates are high, the Eurocurrency markets can still help almost any creditworthy borrower to find a lender of Eurodollars and usually at favorable terms. Moreover, Eurocurrency loans are flexible in their terms, conditions, covenants and currencies.

With regard to currencies, this is particularly important for those companies interested in managing their exposure to exchange risk. For example, it is possible to borrow in any number of different currencies. Regardless of which currency you originally borrowed, it is possible at each rollover date to switch one currency to another. This way companies can match their currency inflows and outflows so as to reduce their exchange risk.

Firms can also reduce their taxes by using offshore banks. A firm can establish a banking affiliate in a tax haven country. The firm can lend funds at relatively low interest rates and borrow from that affiliate at relatively high interest rates. In this case, the affiliate that lends funds to the offshore bank is going to be taxed on the interest it earns, but that interest will be relatively low. The affiliate that borrows funds from the offshore bank controlled by the firm receives a tax deduction on that interest, and the offshore banking affiliate itself is not taxed. Thus, in effect, one can transfer profits from relatively high tax nations to relatively low tax nations.

By using offshore banks one can also reduce the first of currency controls. You can use offshore banks to arrange parallel loans whereby, for example, a company located in Brazil, which has excess cruzeiros that it cannot convert into dollars, can lend those cruzieros to the affiliate or another company located in Brazil. It is possible as well to have a reverse loan of dollars, say, in the United States. In effect, the affiliate of Corporation A in Brazil lends cruzieros to Corporation B while Corporation B in the U.S. lends a parallel amount of dollars to Corporation A in the U.S. So while one cannot convert cruzieros or other block currency into a hard currency, one can deposit indirectly through the medium of a multinational offshore bank.

In a somewhat similar fashion, you can reduce currency control risks. Instead of lending funds directly to an affiliate in, for example, Brazil, where funds are blocked, you can lend money indirectly to that affiliate by first lending the money to an offshore bank. The offshore bank in turn lends the money to your affiliate in Brazil (or whatever country in which you fear the possibility of currency controls) and in this way you have provided funds to your affiliate, but with lower risks.

The countries which are most likely to impose exchange controls are just those countries that must get along with international banks. They are much less likely to impose strict restrictions on the repayment of loans to international banks than to impose restrictions on the repayment of loans back to a parent corporation. This type is known as a back-to-back loan or link financing.

In addition to the advantages for borrowers just mentioned, offshore banking offers numerous advantages to lenders as well. For example, lenders can earn a higher return on funds and can reduce their taxes. Lenders can reduce political risks. This is of particular concern to a buyer of investments in countries where there is the possibility of currency controls or the outright expropriation of wealth. Lenders can also reduce purchasing-power risks. This relates to the risk that a currency you are investing in may suffer significant loss due to inflation. The lender has a wide range of currencies in which to invest, and clearly the dollar is not necessarily the best currency at all times to maintain your purchasing power. By investing in the Eurocurrency markets, one has the ability to access other currencies, and that possibility is denied in domestic markets.

Powers and Benefits of Offshore Banking —For Banks

by Jerome Schneider

To help you understand the powers and benefits of an offshore-bank setup by individuals or corporations, I would like to mention six of the most important advantages. First, the biggest benefit I can think of is that of raising capital. In accepting deposits a bank basically is borrowing from the public, but in effect it is raising capital under a new name. Thus, an offshore bank is probably the best vehicle through which one can raise capital in the international market.

Second, there are tax benefits associated with bank ownership. The banking industry is a protected species under the tax laws and there are certain tax advantages available. An example would be the fact that the income earned by a bank does not involve taxation of the owners.

A third reason is confidentiality. If you are developing a client relationship and that client prefers not to be known to a third party or does not wish to be widely known in general, your transaction with that client is protected by a wall of silence by virtue of offshore bank secrecy laws. Another client-related benefit is the bank's ability to issue guarantees and letters of credit to third parties.

A fourth benefit is the bank's ability to legally avoid currency reporting requirements. As the bank operates from a base outside the U.S., this allows you to get currency into the banking system without reporting it to U.S. authorities, and it is perfectly legal.

Another benefit is cash management. By setting up an offshore bank, a corporation can centralize its cash under its own bank instead of putting its money in a third-party bank. By virtue of that, the corporation can use its money to apportion funds to its cash-needed subsidiaries from its cash-rich subsidiaries. The surplus funds can go out and earn whatever is available in the market through marketing funds or T-bills.

The final benefit I will mention is the individual's or corporation's ability to actually profit from the banking business itself. A good example is the Dow Chemical Corporation that owns an offshore bank in Switzerland and earns profits from that bank's business.

Next, I would like you to consider both the site and the relative ease of establishing an offshore bank, for there are activities allowed offshore that are not permitted in the U.S. Among these would be the absence of insurance requirements that ordinarily apply in the U.S. Also, we are talking about more relaxed requirements for entering into the banking business. By contrast, applying for a bank charter in the United States involves a lot of red tape and many attendant regulations.

It is also possible, in certain jurisdictions, for a bank to issue bearer shares. A bearer share is a certificate, the ownership of which can be transferred from one person to the next without the recording of a name or the use of a transfer agent. You may know that this is a significant matter in raising capital in Europe. For there are European investors and lenders who only want bearer shares because they want to avoid the trouble of registering their names and having to go through the transfer process.

Another benefit derives from tax treaties certain countries have with the U.S. Basically, a tax treaty enables a person paying money to an offshore bank to avoid paying a 30 percent withholding tax on interest payments. Without such a treaty, the U.S. requires that on an interest payment to an offshore bank, 30 percent gets withheld at its source. The Netherlands Antilles is an example of one offshore bank that has such a tax treaty with the U.S. and therefore does not have any interest payments withheld.

A lot of you may be asking, "Why should I go out and bank offshore when I can bank in the United States and be certain my money is safe and protected by FDIC?" Well, one of the misconceptions is that you cannot keep the money of an offshore bank in an insured FDIC account in the U.S. or in a U.S. possession or territory which is covered by FDIC. So, you do not lose that particular insurance.

Considering the site of an offshore bank, the ability to use lawyers and accountants who are established, like the Big Eight accounting firms, is a very important reason for operating from a developed financial center. Such a center is also a necessity for good communication systems, such as mail, telephone and telex. These are extremely important for offshore business, for such business has to be transacted quickly. If you are operating with a time lag and you cannot get your message through, you might lose a significant amount of time in conducting your transactions. Also, you should look for a banking center with good airports and well-traveled routes to the U.S. This will allow you to travel easily if you need to meet with your board of directors or shareholders.

Again, considering the ease of establishing an offshore bank, the process offshore not only involves less red tape, it is also less expensive than in the U.S. The cost entry for acquiring a bank in the U.S. might be as high as $2 million to $10 million—with as little as $500,000 in very rare situations. But if you want to establish an offshore bank, you can do it for as little as $25,000. Moreover, no previous banking experience is required. The expertise you have as a businessman to conduct financial transactions would suffice for you to run an offshore bank.

Still another benefit of offshore banking is that the bank can make investments free of federal regulations, such as commodity investments that may be deemed imprudent by U.S. banks. Because of restrictions from the Glass-Steagle Act, U.S. banks cannot engage in underwriting, but offshore banks do have the power to engage in the underwriting business. Some of you might be interested in captive insurance. For the price of the bank, you might procure insurance because the offshore bank could act as an insurance company. You could also act as a real estate broker, for with the bank you can purchase real estate as a principal as opposed to being in the debt position.

As a final point, I will mention some of the disadvantages of offshore banking. One of the more apparent risks leads to the advice that you should rely on a good bank or one with a good name. You want to make sure you have a bank like Chase Manhattan as the clearing bank or hosting bank that services your offshore facility, as opposed to some banks you have never heard of.

Another risk is political stability. For example, if Cuba takes over the Cayman Islands or takes over one of the colonies, your loan is jeopardized. That is an act of expropriation and it is one of the things you have to be concerned about. One way to avoid that risk is to select jurisdictions which have an impeccable rating for political stability.

How To Bank, Borrow and Invest Outside the U.S.—For Individuals

by Adrian Day

A lot of people think that opening an offshore bank account is very difficult, perhaps involving flying to Switzerland or something of that nature. But it is really a very simple procedure.

One method, if the bank you want has a branch in the United States, is simply to contact the bank's local branch to set up an account at an offshore in the U.S.

If the bank you are interested in does not have a branch in the U.S., you can write to the bank and establish the account through the mail. If you want to establish an account in a typical Swiss bank, for example, you simply send your name, address and type of account desired. The bank will send you a packet of forms, usually about twenty pages in length, which you fill out and return along with a specimen of your signature that has been verified by the Swiss consul. That is all that is involved and you do not even have to leave your house.

One thing to consider, though, is whether you wish the account to be absolutely private and confidential (which are the code words for illegal) or whether you want the account to be normally private and confidential and perfectly legal. If you wish to have assets abroad out of reach and out of the knowledge of the U.S. government, then writing to a Swiss bank and receiving a packet of forms is not the way to go about it.

In such a case, you would normally have to make a personal visit to the bank or its branch of your choice. For example, you could visit Bank Lloyd in the Bahamas and set up an account in Bank Lloyd's Switzerland branch, so you would not have to visit Switzerland yourself.

Some considerations for opening an account apply to the way you send money abroad. If you do not mind the U.S. government knowing about it, sending money abroad is not very difficult. But if we do not wish to report that income, then we have to resort to different means for sending the money. Each of the ways of sending or receiving money from abroad without the government's knowledge involves some kind of cost in terms of time, inconvenience or money, and they all have some risk attached to them. But let me briefly mention some of the main methods.

One approach would be to mail a check abroad, sending it to an individual banker's name and with the address of the bank, but omitting the name of the bank so as not to arouse suspicion. As you may know, the IRS puts mail checks on mail going in and out of the country. So, to the greatest possible degree, you want to avoid anything on an envelope that attracts attention. The check, of course, will come back to the U.S., so there will be some paper record, but depending on the amount of the check it will not necessarily be reported to the U.S. government.

Another common method is to send cash abroad, but frankly I do not recommend this method at all. Even if you insure the cash, it is a very risky practice. You can, instead, send a bank wire abroad. Again, if it is not over $10,000, no report is made. There will be records kept by your bank, but there will be no automatic reporting to the government.

In general, to avoid reporting of such transactions, what you want is to limit the paper trail as much as possible— although you can never eliminate it completely. By limiting the amount of a transaction, it is probable that your bank's record of the check will be lost in an absolute mountain of paperwork. So unless the government is specifically investigating you for some offense, it is unlikely that your check will be noticed.

Another method for sending money abroad is to mail a cashier's check. You should request a notary for each check so your name does not appear on the check. In this case, you should let the receiving bank know that the check is coming from you and specify what should be done with it.

Still another method is to make a personal visit to your bank and carry with you a bank wire or cashier's check, which is not reported as you leave the country. Or you can carry a marketable commodity with you, such as gold, silver or diamonds. You can also send money abroad by using a courier service. But I generally do not recommend this because it is very expensive, and if privacy is a goal, you are entrusting a great deal to a total stranger who has no particular reason to protect you.

The final method I will mention is simply to use Western Union. It is a common way of sending money domestically or abroad. It is simple, quick, relatively inexpensive, and very private. You do not have to provide your name or address when you send the money, and there is a provision on the form when you send the money for a test question to secure identification of the recipient. So there is very little risk involved and there is no paper trail that brings it back to you, for your name is not mentioned anywhere. With this method you can mail abroad more than $5,000, and even though the $5,000 is reported it is not reported to anyone in particular, since you did not use your name.

All of these methods for sending money can also be used for receiving money from abroad. Plus, there are a few additional points that I would like to mention for your information. First, if you do have funds abroad that you want to bring back and use in the U.S., one strategy would be to have your bank purchase negotiable instruments for you, such as municipal bonds. These will be mailed to you and you simply sell them when they arrive. That money would not be reported.

A second strategy would be for the bank to purchase unreportable commodities, like gold or silver, which have low commissions and low premiums. These can be mailed to you, but that is expensive. Instead, you could rely on a computer entry and then pick up the gold or silver in your bank's U.S. branch.

If you do not need the funds here in the U.S. and you have reached that stage in life where you have assets you want to dispose of instead of build up, another method would simply be to use your funds abroad for foreign expenses. If, for example, you wish to travel, then you can obtain a foreign exchange card for purchases worldwide, and you can request that statements not be mailed to you but held by the bank. If you do this, you have to keep very accurate expense records yourself, but there is no paper trail back to the U.S.

Finally, regarding taxes, if you wish to be legal with your offshore account, obviously the tax requirements are the same as for onshore funds. You pay tax on the interest as you would in the U.S., and the deductions are exactly the same, with minor exceptions because of the currency effect. You also have to pay tax on any capital gains due to the appreciation of currency, or you can have the deduction if the foreign currency goes down in value.

How to Bank, Borrow and Invest Outside the U.S.—For Corporations

by Dr. Alan Shapiro

There are three principal depository instruments in the Eurocurrency. These are time deposits, certificates of deposit and floating rate notes. To help you understand them, I will explain the advantages and disadvantages of each.

A time deposit is an ordinary bank deposit whereby you contract to put investments of money for fixed lengths of time, from seven days to six months. The advantages include higher interest rates because banks are willing to pay you more money since your deposit is for a fixed length of time. There is also a minimum of paperwork involved. There is even flexibility with the withdrawal of funds. If you invested for six months and it happens that you need the money after three months, banks are usually willing to allow you to withdraw the money after they adjust the rate to reflect a three-month deposit.

The disadvantages include the fact that your investment is less liquid since it is really up to the bank as to whether you can withdraw your money early. Also, there is no secondary market.

Certificates of deposit (CDs), on the other hand, are more liquid and you have a large and active secondary market. In other words, you receive an actual certificate and you can sell the certificate in the market prior to maturity. On CDs there are no taxes charged or deducted by the issuing bank. You are also not subject to U.S. tax unless you are a citizen or resident. For those of you who have foreign affiliates that choose to invest in the Eurodollar market, your foreign affiliates are not U.S. citizens and, consequently, they are not taxed on the interest on the CDs until that money is brought back to the U.S.

You also have a good deal of flexibility in terms of the maturity of the investment. The maturity on CDs range from call and overnight to five years or more. You also earn a higher return than on U.S. CDs. The interest rate might be on the order of, say, 25 basis points or so greater than on U.S. CDs.

Concerning the disadvantages, Eurodollar CDs are less liquid than CDs in the domestic market. While there is an active secondary market, it is not quite as large as in the United States and, moreover, normally to get the best rate you have to buy a CD on the order of several million dollars. If you want to liquidate the CD or sell it in the secondary market prior to maturity, you will probably have to take somewhat of a discount on it.

With a CD, you will earn a lower rate than on Eurodollar time deposits. Approximately 1/8 of 1 percent less, that is, 12-1/2 basis lower rate. That is the tradeoff because you have less liquidity risk.

A relatively new instrument is known as the floating rate note. This pays a variable interest rate. Usually this rate is adjusted every six months and it is based on the London Interoffice Rate (LIBOR), the rate at which the banks in London trade deposits among each other.

The floating rate note provides an inflation hedge in that as inflation speeds up and interest rates jump, the interest rate on the floating rate note will usually be adjusted to reflect that inflation. This is an advantage compared to being locked into a long-term fixed rate note.

Normally, you are also guaranteed a minimum rate, either for the entire term of the note or for a certain period at the beginning of the note. For example, with a five-year note, you might be guaranteed a minimum of 12 percent for the first two years.

The disadvantages include the fact that you cannot lock in a high rate. If you believe rates are going to come down, then a floating rate note is obviously not for you. Also, the return is uncertain. You are never sure from one period to another what the interest rate will be.

However, I have to point out that what matters is not the interest rate you receive but the purchase power of the returns that you earn, that is, the inflation-adjusted returns. If interest rates jump and you are locked into a five-year, fixed-rate CD, then you are going to suffer a loss. Furthermore, you cannot just look at interest rates alone. For example, should you invest in a 6 percent Swiss franc or a 17 percent U.S. dollar. You cannot say the 6 percent is less than the 17 percent, for the Swiss francs maintain their purchasing power more than dollars. So the 6 percent Swiss franc could return more than your return on a 17 percent U.S. dollar. Again, you cannot just compare interest rates in different currencies. You have to take into account the possibility of currency changes. You also have to take into account how these returns vary with inflation.

Moving now from investing to borrowing, there are several advantages of borrowing in the international money market. First, there are less restrictive convenants. Eurobanks are typically less bureaucratic about their loans. You have the ability to manage exchange risk by rolling over loans denominated in one currency into loans denominated in one or several other currencies.

You can also receive better rates. This is due to the nature of competition in the Eurocurrency market and the fact that banking costs are lower. You also have all-in-the-rate price. You do not have any of these various practices used by domestic banks to jack up interest rates above the stated rate. Specifically, I am referring to such practices as compensating balance requirements, delays on transfers and the like. You do not have any of that when you are borrowing in the Eurocurrency market. So the rate that you see is just what you pay, with no tricks or gimmicks. This is because there are no regulations that force them to earn higher rates by various tricks.

Among the most distinguishing characteristics of Eurocurrency loans are loans made on the basis of floating rate. The amount of money you borrow and the length of time of the loan are set, but the interest rate itself varies. Typically, the loan is rolled over every six months, and rate pricing is based on LIBOR plus a certain percent. As LIBOR changes, so will your cost of funds, but the change is typically only every six months.

Another characteristic of Eurocurrency loans is speed. They do things quickly in the market, to the point where you can have money within several days of your request.

The maturity of loans can vary from a few months to seven to ten years. Their size is enormous, from less than a million to over a billion dollars. You also have a good deal of flexibility regarding special conditions and covenants. You have multicurrency clauses which enable you to roll over your loan from one currency to another at every six-month period.

Among these special features and clauses in Eurocurrency loans, one is the cancellation clause. This gives the borrower or lender the option to cancel the loan at any rollover date. Typically, every six months.

There is also a clause to cover general increases in the lender's costs, such as, if the U.S. Goverment imposes Regulation M on Eurocurrency loans to force banks to hold reserves against deposits; this, of course, raises the cost of funding loans.

There typically is a special availability clause which gives the bank the right to call for prepayment of the loan if sufficient dollar funds are not available in the Eurodollar market. There is a prepayment clause which gives the borrower the right to prepay the loan, possibly with a penalty.

A very important factor is the jurisdiction. The loan contract will state under what jurisdiction any disputes between the borrower and lender are settled. This is important because there are significant differences, between say the U.S. and U.K., with regard to loans. There is also a tax clause which gives banks the right to pass on any higher taxes levied on them to borrowers.

There is also a commitment fee. That is, you usually have a draw-down schedule whereby you can draw down so much in each time period. The amount you do not draw down, you pay the commitment fee, normally one-half of 1 percent annually.

It should be clear that many of the special clauses that I have gone over reflect attempts to stay clear of even remotely possible political risks, such as the availability clause, cancellation clause and the like.

To conclude, as you can see, there are some real advantages to borrowing and lending in the Eurocurrency markets.

How to Bank, Borrow and Invest Outside the U.S.—For Banks

by Jerome Schneider

There are two types of offshore banks. One we can refer to as a Street Bank, having a teller, a vault, and a paying and receiving window. Such a bank has an A license and the cost of setting up an A Bank is considerable—at least $250,000 per year to maintain.

The other type of bank is a B Bank, sometimes called a Brass Plate Bank or Nameplate Bank because it may be no more than a nameplate at a trust company. But to the outside world, this type of bank is just as sophisticated and just as well known in the international community as an A Bank. One of the benefits of a B Bank is its inexpensiveness. For example, you do not have to buy or rent a building to maintain the bank and you can even use the existing staff at the trust company instead of hiring and training your own staff.

A key issue for a B Bank is the board of directors behind the nameplate. For legal purposes, so transactions are not a sham, there has to be a seat of management outside the U.S. If that board of directors is not outside the U.S., you can be accused of operating a banking business in the U.S. without a license.

To understand how a B Bank operates, a common initial question is "Where is all the money kept?" The answer is that an offshore bank can deposit money in any bank in the world. It can obtain the equivalent of a corporate checking account at the Bank of America or a Swiss bank or any other bank. The offshore bank can also maintain a relationship with an institution that is just a safe deposit to keep cash or bullion or whatever.

The next question is "How does the day-to-day business of the bank work?" Basically, the person in the U.S. delegates authority to act for the bank to conduct day-to-day business. This might be a power of attorney to perform limited business. Again, if the person here is doing all the decision making then you really do not have an offshore bank; you have a sham. So it is very important that if any business needs to be conducted, such as making a deposit, the information has to be passed to the offshore board of directors. The directors then meet, resolve the piece of business, and the authority is passed back to the U.S. Depending on how you structure the delegation of authority to the board of directors, you can preserve the benefits of doing business offshore and still maintain a certain amount of authority.

A related issue is "How do you communicate with the offshore bank?" We can rely on any of four basic ways of communicating with your bank offshore. First, you can write a letter to the board of directors instructing them, for example, to "Please buy 500 shares of GM stock." The problem, though, is that the stock's price might go down by the time the teller reaches the bank. A second method would be to use the telex, which is much faster. This method consists of sending teletype information to the bank's directors, then the board effects the piece of business offshore. The telephone, of course, is the quickest way of communicating with the bank, and that is why having a good communications system between the offshore bank and the U.S. is so important. But the disadvantage with the telephone is that you have no way of proving the identity of the person who is calling. Therefore, a telephone call should be followed up by a letter or a telex or secret communication.

The fourth communications approach is a way we have found to be very effective for many of our clients for whom we have set up offshore banks. This is a telecopier arrangement whereby a document can be instantly transmitted over the phone line in the course of six minutes either way. So if you wanted to issue a loan commitment or whatever, the document would be prepared by your board of directors offshore and an exact copy of the document simply transmitted to you, the intermediary, in the U.S.

How Offshore Banking Works
by Thomas Bayer

For private banks owned offshore, probably the single biggest use is for group transactions. Several examples can illustrate how these transactions operate and their advantages.

One is back-to-back, whereby relatively low interest is paid to bank depositors while higher interest is charged for loans. The spread between these two interest rates is the source of the bank's tax-free profit.

Centralized cash management is another advantageous banking practice for a corporation that has divisions around the world. The corporation can take the idle cash balances or liquidity out of the various members of the group and pool them into their own offshore bank to create round lots for possible investment in foreign currency markets. This practice has the triple advantages of higher net earnings for the total group, an income which is tax free in the bank's hands, and income which would not have been earned due to the idleness of the small cash balances in the different group companies. This option for corporations is potentially available to individuals as well. There are corporations that have many clients with relatively small assets, say $20,000 to $30,000; and by pooling these funds into round lots of a half-million or million dollars, the corporation can make an investment in Euro or Asian currency markets. This allows the individual clients to earn the otherwise unobtainable high interest on these currency markets.

A third practice is the discounting of group receivables. Let us suppose that a U.S. company is owed $100,000 by a European company that has bought a product from them. The U.S. company can discount that receivable off to its affiliated offshore bank at, say, $90,000. This reduces the company's profit but provides the bank a profit when the $100,000 payment is received. If the debtor is shaky or doubtful, it is also possible to discount the debt to your private bank, not in exchange for cash, but for a debt due from your bank. This has the effect of changing your debtor from an arm's length person about whom you are unsure of collectibility to a bank of which you are sure of the collectibility. Finally, if the debt goes bad, the offshore bank has recourse back to the original company which discounted it. So the loss is retransferred back onshore to the U.S. company.

Still another practice is for the offshore bank to function as a third-party guarantor to group borrowings within operating companies. As the offshore bank establishes its own status and credibility, it may come to pass that the company itself might not have as high a credit rating as the offshore bank. So with the bank's guarantee on a borrowing application, the borrowing company may be able to reduce its interest rate onshore. The offshore bank can also help by providing letters of credit and group financing. The setup costs and management fees for obtaining that line of credit may be the same with the offshore bank as with an onshore bank, but the key difference is that you are paying the interest to yourself if that line of credit comes from your own offshore bank instead of an outside bank.

In offshore banking there are many advantageous practices beyond those for group transactions just mentioned. One to consider is that of placing funds in the Euro and Asian currency markets. Because there is no withholding tax charged in these currency markets, you have a situation with no withholding tax on the part of the borrowing bank and no income tax for your offshore bank. Similarly, you might invest in Euro bonds and debentures, which are simply an extension of the interest-bearing deposits. They are, of course, for a longer period of time and their value is floating up and down according to the world bond market, but again there is no withholding tax involved.

Another thing to consider is that if you can obtain or command 14 or 15 percent interest on your deposits in the U.S., your offshore bank is able to get that same interest rate. As you normally command a premium that can have no tax through the offshore bank, you are really at 28 percent to 30 percent equivalent gross. If you can obtain that sort of yield just on deposits, why take the risk of making other types of direct investments?

Next you might consider portfolio investment on world share markets. It is common for private banks to invest in shares, but if you are in the U.S. you must appoint a custodian somewhere close to effect your settlement. In the South Pacific, for example, we use a custodian based in Canada; this can be through any one of the public trustee companies in Canada who physically hold the script in their name and settle against U.S. purchases and sales. The offshore bank might appoint you or your own personal investment advisor to advise the bank on what purchases or sales are to be made. The final decision is made by the bank's board of directors in the offshore locale, but commercial reality indicates that generally they would follow your choice.

Through offshore banking, still another option available to you is that of making deposits in currency other than U.S. dollars. You can see the profitability in this by considering, for example, that Australian dollars are yielding 19% on 30-day money. But you should approach this carefully, for although this is a way to increase your income, it also exposes you to potential movements in exchange rates. So you must be prepared to assess and discuss such exchange exposure with the managers of your offshore bank. To give a very extreme example, recently the Internal Bank in Vanuatu and Europe offered up to 55 percent interest on French francs for 30-day money. Obviously, everyone in Europe panicked that the French franc might devalue. Yet, you must consider that if you are going to get 55 percent, you can withstand a substantial devaluation and still come out ahead. It is these sorts of opportunities in other currencies that generally are not thought about by persons in the United States. I mention this because your whole mentality may be geared to the U.S. dollar, and you should realize that there are other currencies that can allow you to increase your yield.

Another potential with offshore banking is to invest on the float. This involves the fact that most offshore jurisdictions do not have automatic clearing facilities and, instead, have a manual clearing situation which can result in weeks or months for a check to clear. You have the potential with a local Street Bank of having your money on call earning interest. Thereby, when the check finally clears and is sent back for presentation, the local bank will automatically take the money off call and honor the check. You cannot be writing checks without coverage, of course, but you can be earning interest while your check is waiting to be presented—and this could be a substantial amount when the check is very large.

There are some people who want to be in the banking business. An advantage of going into offshore banking is that it gives you an easy point of entry and enables you to develop management and a track record so you can ultimately open bank branches in other taxable jurisdictions. However, I make a caveat that when you go into this sort of business, you need risk management and lending expertise. You should not necessarily depend upon your representatives in the offshore locale because that kind of expertise may not be there.

Offshore banking can also help you facilitate trade. If you have an offshore bank and you are doing business, you can provide letters of credit and you can make arm's length loans and mortgages. I would note that lending back into the U.S. runs into the 30 percent withholding tax, but you can also lend into countries like Australia and New Zealand that are stable and have very low withholding taxes. For example, in New Zealand, although there is a 15 percent withholding tax, we have never failed to receive an exemption from this withholding tax from the reserve bank in New Zealand. So the full amount of interest comes out of New Zealand without any deduction, and this income is earned tax free in your offshore bank.

With an offshore bank you are also capable of receiving deposits from the public. You do need a soundly based bank with proven management, however. If you want to attract deposits, you have to pay a premium on those deposits since you are an unknown and competing against the world name banks. Paying that premium means that you have to utilize those funds in a manner that generates sufficiently high interest for you to make a profit, and this takes real expertise. I do not recommend this to people just getting into the banking business, for if you are intending to lend money from yourself and borrow from the public, that is the fastest way I know to financial collapse.

The last point I want to mention is the not uncommon practice of owning an offshore bank to fulfill a dream. There is status attached to saying, "I own a foreign bank." Those people are not necessarily silly, though they may just be doing it for status, for they are also making an investment. As years go by, it becomes increasingly difficult to obtain bank licenses; moreover, laws are passed in onshore jurisdictions, making it harder for their residents to go into offshore business. So if a person has an offshore bank now, he is effectively investing in the future. That is, the person buys it today for the status, but the offshore bank is there like an insurance policy when it's needed.

Owning an Offshore Bank: New Profit Center for the '80s

by Jerome Schneider

At a time when industry is turning to dust, the one single industry that has shown profits each year has been international banking. Moreover, according to a recent survey, the banking industry as a whole has paid a negative 2 percent in tax. That means through the use of tax credits of one form or another, banks have had government owing them money while industry has paid an average of 50 percent on tax.

Why have bankers profited so much and become so successful? The key to commodity banking is money. Based upon our economy, there is always somebody that needs money, good times or bad, so the service offered by banks is always in demand. Banking is always potentially profitable, since banking in itself is borrowing cheap from depositors and lending high. Furthermore, banking is not labor-intensive. Banking is relatively impervious to competition, as there are just a few bankers in comparison to the number of other industries.

The next question is, "If banking is so profitable, why isn't everybody doing it?" Banking for a great period of time has been a closed fraternity. According to the Federal Reserve, only persons who are involved in a corporation that owns a U.S. bank can actually own other U.S. banks. Another problem with getting into U.S. banking is its costliness. If you were lucky enough to get a bank, it would cost you $2 million or up to $25 million. So it is a very expensive proposition.

A viable alternative to banking in the U.S. is offshore banking, for it overcomes many of the restrictive problems one encounters in the U.S. The cost of an offshore bank, for example, is about $25,000. It is also relatively easy to own, since you do not need the type of banking experience required to establish a bank in the U.S.

Offshore banks also provide more benefits than one would obtain by setting up a U.S. bank. For example, in-house transactions are possible, whereby you make bank transactions, such as loans, with yourself. The bank offers the ability to recycle dollars through the Euromarket. The bank also can act as an insurance company, which is an activity prohibited in the U.S. Finally, offshore banks do not have to pay taxes on their banking profits as do U.S. banks.

Turning now to how offshore banks can be profit centers, the basic point is that essentially there are three ways banks can make money: (1) by taking deposits; (2) extending credit; and (3) investing. With regard to taking deposits, there are three methods for offshore banks. The first is the non-U.S. advertising method. You cannot advertise your banking business in the U.S. media because of provisions in the banking laws. But you can accept deposits from the U.S. public, and you can advertise to that public through non-U.S. publications such as the *International Herald-Tribune* or the Latin-American edition of *Time* magazine.

The second method is the Euromarket placement method. This basically involves having a bank issue a set amount of certificates of deposit for an offshore bank, subsequently placing them with a broker in Europe. The broker then places the certificates of deposit with his clients whose portfolios indicated an interest in earning favorable rates of return.

The third method for taking deposits is private solicitation. This involves your ability to contact people in the U.S. without making a public offering or doing what is called the doing-business-requirement test. In other words, if an associate, employee or acquaintance of yours personally invites another person to make a deposit into your bank, that does not trigger any regulator concern in the U.S. It is considered private solicitation.

The next area of profit-making for an offshore bank is that of extending credit. There are four basic instruments used in extending credit. First is a letter of credit, which is a financial instrument saying that if certain conditions are met, then payment will be rendered. Second is a bank guarantee, which is a financial instrument that can guarantee a loan. Secured lending is another profitable area. Then there is the back-to-back loan whereby you accept a person's deposit and then relend him a certain amount for an onward transaction he has. Thus, the person's deposit is collateral for the loan.

The third area of profit-making for a bank is investing—and as mentioned previously, an offshore bank can invest in many different types of things that ordinarily are prohibited for U.S. banks. Some examples of investments would be securities, commodities, and real estate as a principal.

To conclude, we can examine ten cases where offshore banks are offering profitability. The first case is the American Express International Banking Corporation. American Express is not a bank for U.S. bank purposes and it has no banks in the U.S. It does have a bank set up in London, along with offices in Hong Kong and the Cayman Islands. American Express International Bank provides business and financial institutions and governments a wide choice of international financing services such as short-term working capital, term and project financing, collections, deposits and money transfer services. According to published reports, from 1976 to 1979, American Express International Bank returned to American Express a minimum of $30 million per year net profit.

The next case is Dow Banking Corporation, owned by Dow Chemical Corporation in Michigan and based in Switzerland. This is a unique example because Dow is an industry corporation and it owns a subsidiary called Dow Overseas. They are involved with portfolio management and financial accommodations for international transactions. From 1976 to 1979, Dow Banking returned to Dow Chemical an average of $60 million per year.

A third example is Merrill Lynch, with an offshore bank in London and Panama started in 1976. It does trading and Eurodollar financing.

The fourth case is Bank Firestone, started by the Firestone Tire and Rubber Company in 1965 and dissolved in 1975. Bank Firestone was involved with in-house transactions as well as with third parties. Bank Firestone held gold for the Firestone Corporation back in 1974 and 1975, when it was illegal to hold gold in onshore banks. It was an effort to avoid some U.S. requirements on gold ownership, and the Justice Department sued them to recover $62 million in penalties. But in a recent verdict, Firestone was found not guilty.

The last six cases involved some of our clients, and I will go through them quickly. One client used his bank as an escrow company for land sales and deals with Europeans. His benefit is in terms of tax treatment, for if an escrow is held between buyer and seller there is no tax due.

Another client makes loans to third parties, referrals, and buys and sells stocks on the New York and American Stock Exchanges. By using his own bank, he effectively eliminates or avoids the U.S. capital gains tax on those transactions.

One client who is heavily industrialized has been able to come up with large sources of capital in Europe and he finds American banks interested in borrowing the money. He has wedged his bank in as an intermediary, and to date he has made $25 million in commissions, which are tax-free through his bank.

Another client has used his bank for the value of a bank letterhead in his direct mailing. Before establishing his bank, he received a one percent response on his mailings, but afterwards he got a 10 percent response to his solicitations. Evidently, people listen to banks as opposed to corporations.

One client was heavily involved with a divorce. He had assets all over the world and wanted to put them in a safe haven by means of establishing his own bank. I believe that an offshore bank is one of the most effective ways to camouflage assets because the idea of individual ownership is not readily associated with a bank.

The next case is a banker who is a member of a country club. Others at his country club have deposited $100,000 each in his offshore bank. They borrow on a revolving credit basis and are receiving accrued interest on their certificates of deposit tax-free.

The last case involves an individual who ran an ad in the *International Herald-Tribune* and *Time* to obtain depositors for his offshore bank. The ad cost about $500 and the amount of deposits he received was in excess of $100,000. With this and all the other examples in mind, I think you can see that offshore banks are viable profit centers and that the banking industry no longer has to be a closed fraternity.